TOP
RAILWAY
JOURNEYS
OF THE WORLD

'*Herein, I think, lies the chief attraction of railway travel. The speed is so easy, and the train disturbs so little the scenes through which it takes us, that our heart becomes full of the placidity and stillness of the country; and while the body is borne forward in the flying chain of carriages, the thoughts alight, as the humour moves them, at unfrequented stations; they make haste up the poplar alley that leads toward the town; they are left behind with the signalman as, shading his eyes with his hand, he watches the long train sweep away into the golden distance.*'

From An Ordered South
Robert Louis Stevenson

TOP
RAILWAY
JOURNEYS
OF THE WORLD

TOM SAVIO

NEW HOLLAND

This edition published 2013

First published in 2001 by New Holland Publishers
LONDON ● CAPE TOWN ● SYDNEY ● AUCKLAND

www.newhollandpublishers.com

Garfield House, 86–88 Edgware Road, London, W2 2EA, United Kingdom
Wembley Square First Floor Solan Road Gardens Cape Town 8001 South Africa
Unit 1, 66 Gibbes Street, Chatswood, NSW 2067, Australia
218 Lake Road, Northcote, Auckland, New Zealand

ISBN 9781780095097

Although the publishers have made every effort to ensure that information
contained in this book was meticulously researched and correct at the time of going
to press, they accept no responsibility for any inaccuracies, loss,
injury or inconvenience sustained by any person using this book as reference.

A catalogue record of this book is available at the British Library and at the National Library of Australia

DESIGNER KEISHA GALBRAITH
EDITORS INGRID SCHNEIDER & SIMON POOLEY
COMMISSIONING EDITOR SIMON POOLEY
MANAGING EDITORS CLAUDIA DOS SANTOS & MARI ROBERTS
MANAGING ART EDITOR PETER BOSMAN
CARTOGRAPHER JOHN LOUBSER
PICTURE RESEARCHER SONYA MEYER
PROOFREADER/INDEXER GILL GORDON
CONSULTANT LAURIE MARSHALL
PRODUCTION MYRNA COLLINS

PRINTED BY Toppan Leefung Printing Ltd

10 9 8 7 6 5 4 3 2 1

Follow New Holland Publishers on Facebook:
www.facebook.com/NewHollandPublishers

PAGE 2: *The luxurious Eastern & Oriental Express travels through lush forest in Thailand.*
RIGHT: *A gangway view of a Norwegian State Railways – Norges Statesbaner – locomotive.*
OVERLEAF: *Despite white-out weather, the Furka-Oberalp Bahn keeps trains running.*
AMERICA (PAGE 14): *A Durango & Silverton Narrow Gauge Railroad train in the Animas Gorge.*
EUROPE (PAGE 44): *Passengers disembark into a wintry landscape in Norway.*
ASIA (PAGE 86): *A train from Peshawar steams towards a Pathan village en route to the Khyber Pass.*
AUSTRALASIA (PAGE 126): *The TranzAlpine train crossing the Bealey River in New Zealand.*
AFRICA (PAGE 140): *The Blue Train travels through the winelands of South Africa's Western Cape.*

CONTENTS

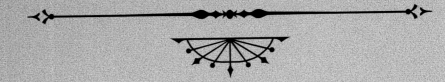

Introduction

THE WORLD'S GREAT RAILWAY JOURNEYS

WELCOME ABOARD! You are about to experience the world's most scenic and adventurous passenger trains right from your comfy club chair – either by travelling vicariously through the chapters of this book, or by using it as a guide to future rail adventures. While you may not encounter intriguing characters in the flesh or see great scenic vistas from your easy chair, the faces of the passengers and the sights along the way conjured in your mind will be uniquely your own and bound only by the limits of your imagination. So, read and enjoy, knowing that you are embarking on the greatest railway journeys – imaginable.

The breadth of my own lifetime of railway travels flashed before me on the inaugural run of the Acela Express high-speed train. A television reporter asked if I could look out the window at 217 kph (135 mph) and tell him exactly where we were and something of its history. Indeed I could – we were negotiating the famous 'S' curve along Amtrak's Northeast Corridor at Elizabeth, New Jersey station. As for the history, I recounted how my avocation as a rail fan, or trainspotter, began from that station 40 years ago. It was there that I met for the first time another enthusiast and learned of the worldwide cadre of rail fans, replete with mysterious protocols and jargon, set on preserving the most environmentally friendly and civilized form of land transport – railways.

My avocation eventually transformed into careers as station-master, railway museum curator, Polish steam engine driver and travel journalist. Then, during one of my Canadian rail adventures, while I was holding forth in a bar in Kamloops,

British Columbia, following a run of the Rocky Mountaineer cruise train, I was dubbed a '19th-century Railway Baron' by a bemused railroad official – and the title has endured.

Before setting out on your own railway journey, there are a few important terms to remember so that you are not spotted as a neophyte on the station platforms and in the engine sheds of the world. They are: locomotives, flanged wheels and track gauges. If you saw Andrew Lloyd Webber's *Starlight Express*, you will know that locomotives, like ice cream, come in three basic flavours and everyone has their favourite –steam, diesel or electric. Electrics are the fastest and most efficient, but they're expensive, look like bricks and are almost silent, so they're rather boring when travelling at less than 290 kph (180 mph). Diesels can barely reach 160 kph (100 mph), are less efficient, also look like bricks, and smell bad besides, so they're not very interesting at all. Steam locomotives on the other hand are even slower, inefficient, dirty and sooty, blow smoke, have whirling wheels, piercing whistles and even clanging bells in North America, so naturally, steam locomotives – like chocolate ice cream – are best.

Railway wheels have flanges on their inside edges to guide them along the tracks and through the tricky turnouts where routes diverge. Contrary to the typical newspaper account, the engine driver does not steer the train; that's what the flanged wheels do. This is not as obvious as it may seem – once, I even had to explain this concept to a railway official who had never looked beneath the train to see how it worked!

Track gauge is the distance between the inside of the two rails. The British standard gauge of 1.435 metres (4 feet 8½ inches) became the world standard because the British were the first to manufacture and export railway technology and nomenclature. This odd measurement probably evolved from a gauge used by British horse wagon makers who also built early railway wagons. Rails that are closer together than standard gauge are called 'narrow gauge' and are typically

---

LEFT: *A merry band of actors recreates a scene from the early days of rail travel in this 1925 celebration of the 100th anniversary of the Stockton & Darlington line, the world's first steam-powered public railway.*

0.914 metres (3 feet) in the United States, 1.067 metres (3 feet 6 inches) or 'Imperial Gauge' in the former British Empire and 1 metre (3 feet 3 inches) in Europe. Due to their smaller scale, narrow-gauge railways are cheaper to build, but carry lighter loads. Tracks wider than standard gauge are called 'broad gauge' and are found principally in Russia, the Iberian Peninsula, the Indian subcontinent and Australia. They can carry greater loads, but they cost more and require more land. Trains of one gauge cannot operate on the tracks of another gauge unless their wheels are changed or another rail is installed. And finally, in America, railway translates as 'railroad' and engine driver as 'engineer'.

In 1825 George Stephenson ignited a revolution in human history when he opened the world's first steam-powered public railway, the Stockton & Darlington, in the north of England. Although primitive 'railways' can be traced back to ancient times – when mineral carts were pushed along rough-hewn guide ways – it wasn't until the early 19th century that railways, propelled by the newly perfected steam locomotive, actually became public conveyances. This enabled natural resources, manufactured goods and the masses of common people to be transported cheaply, rapidly and predictably over long distances via the rail network. Industry, commerce, culture, new ideas and even the gene pool were eventually dispersed in all directions. Railways were the greatest invention of the Industrial Revolution, and the Industrial Revolution was driven faster and further by the railways. It was a perfect synergy.

'Railway mania' eventually took hold of Britain, and competing lines were built without regard to cost or prospective customers, which led to some splendid engineering follies. The most sublime of these nonsense railways was the Settle & Carlisle Line through the wild Pennine hills. Known in legend as 'The Long Drag', it is one of history's great railway epics and rail journeys.

Of course, the British were not the only disciples of monumental railway foolishness. American religious zealot Albert Kinsey Owens promoted what became the heroically named but financially challenged Kansas City, Mexico and Orient Railway. It was conceived to link America's Midwest with Asia – 'diagonally', via Mexico's Pacific coast. Today, only rusty bits and pieces remain north of the Rio Grande, but down south in Mexico, passenger trains still brave 'El Chepe's' 39 bridges, scores of tunnels and circles of track to the brink of Canyon del Cobre – muchos times larger than Arizona's Grand Canyon.

Although railways began in Great Britain, they had their greatest impact in the undeveloped regions of Asia, Africa, Australia and the Americas, where they pioneered the development of natural resources, commerce and cities. In Great Britain, where land and urban development was centuries old, an efficient, albeit unhurried canal system already existed.

Remarkably, a few fascinating and scenic pioneer railways still stalk the mountains of Colorado, New Mexico, Pakistan and India. The Durango & Silverton and the Cumbres & Toltec are the last links to the bonanza railroads that were built in the Rocky Mountains to the cries of 'Silver!' In the dusty, desolate mountains of northwest Pakistan, steam locomotives continue to tramp the giant-sized 1.676-metre (5-foot 6-inch) gauge track up to the top of storied Khyber Pass. But, improbable as their rights-of-way are, these railways were soundly engineered when compared with the precarious Darjeeling Railway. Conceived by the British Raj to reach the balmy uplands during the stifling Indian summer, the diminutive Darjeeling corkscrews up and over itself in the shadow of the Himalayas. However, as high as these mountain-climbing railways go, they are still thousands of feet shy of Peru's Puno-Cusco Line, which boasts a station at 4281 metres (14,046 feet).

Some of these railways were too frail to roll any longer under their own steam. Those that finally give in to clogged flues and arthritic pistons were sometimes redeemed by enthusiasts, who transform them into tourist and museum railways. France's Chemin de Fer du Vivarais has been reborn as a museum railway providing service today through the Rhône Valley vineyards that rivals its heyday a hundred years ago, blurring the line between real and make-believe.

Other routes, such as Norway's Flåmsbanen and Switzerland's Glacier Express, were engineered whimsically from their inceptions, entertaining skiers and tourists with curves, bridges and tunnels to snowy peaks while transporting local passengers, goods and natural resources. Once I remarked to the engine driver of the Glacier Express how amazed I was with the route's many delicate curving viaducts. He replied: 'We Swiss can build proper railways too, but we built this with the tourists in mind.'

RIGHT: *Since the zenith of the railway age the Orient-Express, in its various guises, has been the train by which all other luxury trains are judged.*

The railway builders' true monuments, though, were the transcontinental trunk lines that marched across unbroken ground, interminable deserts and alpine passes linking Atlantic and Pacific Oceans, Pacific and Indian Oceans, and Europe with Asia. They forged nations and empires with steel rails. From the dome cars of The Canadian and the lounge cars of The Indian Pacific, the verdant and varied geography that enriches Canada and the parched, treeless desert that holds Australia captive can be viewed like rolling tableaux. Indeed, some rail routes have become completely identified with a country, particularly the line along 'Old Father Rhine', the majestic river that bonds Germany's cultural contraries, industry and Romanticism. One of the shortest 'transcontinental' rail journeys is New Zealand's TranzAlpine, which twists across South Island from the Pacific to the Tasman Sea. The longest and most culturally diverse railway journey is via the Trans-Siberian and Trans-Mongolian expresses, which link the Old World of Europe with the ancient world of China, spanning 8000 kilometres (5000 miles) and 5000 years of civilization – all for the price of a train ticket.

The Railway Age reached its zenith during the 'Inter-War Period', the years between the world wars. Railway trackage was at its maximum, and the trains their most lavish. The opulent Art Nouveau carriages of the legendary Orient-Express catered alike to European royalty and Balkan anarchists along its route from Paris to Constantinople (Istanbul). In California, the spectacular Daylight chauffeured Hollywood glitterati to William Randolph Hearst's Cuesta Encantada high above the Pacific Ocean. South Africans aboard the Union Limited's cozy Imperial Gauge carriages were comforted with 'hot shower baths and valet service in every

LEFT: *Rovos Rail's steam locomotive Bianca taking on water. Hauling the luxurious* Pride of Africa *cruise train across southern Africa is thirsty work.*

coach'. And across Canada, English 'milords' enjoyed some of the finest scenery in the New World aboard the cars of The Continental Limited, assured that a proper afternoon tea would be served atop Yellowhead Pass. Indeed, passengers onboard the great trains were treated like pampered guests of grand hotels. In the words of Matt Cahoon, Manager, Onboard Services of Amtrak's illustrious Coast Starlight, 'When you are running an overnight train, you are really operating a hotel on wheels, and the passengers are our guests and we treat them as such.'

So, it is not surprising that the impetus for the remarkable rebirth of luxurious railway travel today came from a highly successful hotelier and shipping magnate, James B. Sherwood. Having grown bored with modern business travel, Sherwood brought together a family of romantically historic hotels that were convenient to the ports served by his global firm, Sea Containers Group. He then linked many of his 'properties' with ultra-deluxe express trains in the tradition of Europe's Compagnie Internationale des Wagons-Lits et des Grands Express Europeens.

The Wagons-Lits Company, or 'Madame la Compagnie' to travel cognoscenti, set the world standard for rail travel in 1883, when it first knitted Europe and Asia together with the pleasure carriages of the Orient-Express. Over the decades, 'The Magic Carpet to the East' weathered Europe's fickle political climate; but when it was re-established after the devastation of World War II, it began a slow and steady decline and succumbed to indifference and the jet age in 1977. To be sure, you can still find its celebrated name, but it is an ordinary train that terminates without pomp in Vienna, 1287 kilometres (800 miles) short of its traditional berth beneath the minarets of the Golden Horn.

Soon after its fall from grace, some of Madame la Compagnie's exquisite carriages went on the block in Monte Carlo. With the clap of the auctioneer's gavel, James Sherwood and his wife Shirley became the new keepers of the Orient-Express legend. Those carriages, along with their siblings from the Train Bleu and the Fleche d'Or, etc., were restored by some of the same families of artisans who had originally crafted them. Thus 'The King of Trains' was reborn as the Venice Simplon-Orient-Express (V S-O-E).

On a trip to Paris, the 'Baroness' and I hailed a cab from the Hotel Fleche d'Or and dashed to the Gare de l'Est to board the Venice Simplon-Orient-Express. When the driver asked 'What train do you catch, monsieur?', I replied 'Orient-Express.' 'But of course!' came his reply, affirming that his patrons would naturally be associated with 'the world's most celebrated train'.

The Venice Simplon-Orient-Express engendered the modern cruise train, combining the sumptuously appointed carriages, haute cuisine and ambience of the belle epoque of rail travel, with the varied itineraries and adroit marketing of gala cruise ships. The V S-O-E was followed by the aristocratic Royal Scotsman, conceived by canal cruise entrepreneur Michael Ryan. They were followed by a virtual galaxy of '5-star' trains running on five continents, including the Eastern & Oriental Express down the Malay Peninsula; India's Royal Orient Express; Spain's El Transcantábrico; and Rohan Vos's extraordinary steam-hauled Pride of Africa, tracking the mystical dream of the Cape to Cairo Railway to Victoria Falls and Dar Es Salaam.

Of course, as you will read, not all great railway journeys are all that comfortable or have 'Monsieur Escoffier' tending the restaurant car; nor are you likely to meet a fascinating expatriate onboard. The Beijing to Hanoi route is a benchmark among railway travellers eager to collect 'rare mileage', but its geographical and cultural kaleidoscope is probably best experienced after many other great railway journeys – just as you would climb many other peaks before attempting Everest.

As railways near their second century, and I edit the second edition of this book, one of the trains – Al Andalus – has turned its last wheel, and normal steam-powered trains are dwindling in both Poland and China. However, modern rail triumphs like the Eurotunnel linking Britain and the Continent are bridging ancient cultural chasms that will permanently reshape Western history. Best of all, new trains and railways have become realities, including Wagons-Lits' own Pullman Orient-Express, the extension of The Gahn to Darwin at Australia's 'Top End', and the Tibet-China Railway – by far the highest in the world. So, there are sure to be many great railway journeys in the future. Montez a bord! En voiture! All aboard!

Tom Savio
The Railway Baron

THE AMERICAS

The Canadian

TORONTO TO VANCOUVER

by Pierre Home-Douglas

IT IS A SUNNY MORNING IN early November and hundreds of people are streaming through Toronto's downtown Union Station. Briefcases in hand, they have just emerged from commuter trains that pour into the city every weekday, crammed with office workers from the surrounding suburbs. I'm heading the other way – out to gate nine and train number one on the departure board. Destination: Vancouver, British Columbia, 4451 kilometres (2766 miles) away on the shores of the Pacific Ocean.

I join an eclectic group of travellers at the gate: backpackers, a tour group from the UK, a bevy of retired Americans, Japanese tourists, two Amish couples, and a reasonably-sized contingent of Canadians. Once we reach the platform, the backpacking crowd and a few others head left to the two economy cars at the front of the train. I turn right and hop aboard the Silver & Blue sleeping car service, looking for car 129 – my home for the next three days. One problem; there appears to be no car 129, a mistake with the numbering, I am told. I'm shown to Car 128 instead as we pull out of the station precisely at 09:00. We head past the 553-metre (1814-foot) CN Tower, past Skydome, home to Toronto's professional baseball and football teams, and then out toward the western end of the city. The train picks up speed and I watch as the skyscrapers slowly recede from view and we move into a land of seemingly endless suburbs. In the meantime, things have been sorted out on the accommodation front, so I lay out my gear in my double bedroom. On the western transcontinental Canadian, Via Rail Canada's flagship route, Silver & Blue class

offers a choice of upper and lower berths, as well as single, double, and triple bedrooms and the Romance by Rail package using two double bedrooms en suite with a king-size bed. My room is comfortable but spartan – no rich wood panelling or silk-covered walls here. There are two chairs, a WC, and a small sink. The beds, concealed in the wall, are lowered by a porter at night.

Now that I'm set up I begin exploring my new world. Silver & Blue class patrons have the exclusive use of The Canadian's dining cars, lounges, and the celebrated glass-roofed panorama cars. All of these stainless steel Art Moderne-style cars were introduced in the mid-1950s and drew instant accolades from both railroad aficionados and the general public. *Vogue* magazine devoted most of an issue to the cars' interiors in 1955. In the late 1990s, VIA Rail, Canada's national passenger railway system, invested CAN$200-million in the restoration and upgrading of 185 of the cars. Steam was replaced by electric heat, a shower was added to each sleeping car, and mechanical components, such as the brakes, were overhauled.

I take a seat in one of the four 24-seat dome cars and settle in for a little sightseeing. As the train heads north, the suburbs eventually give way to farmlands. By late morning we have entered a new world of island-dotted lakes. This is part of the Muskoka region, 'cottage country' for Torontonians,

---

ABOVE: *Sharp-eyed observers can occasionally spot moose, deer and red fox from the train's observation cars.*

RIGHT: *The stainless steel Art Moderne cars of* The Canadian *pass Mount Robson, Canada's highest peak, in the majestic Rocky Mountains. The glass-roofed panorama cars are popular spots on the trip and an excellent place to gather for a drink and conversation on a starry night.*

who seek refuge here on weekends and during summer holidays from the hurly-burly of city life. The train slowly wends its way from lake to lake, past cottages with boats tied up by the water's edge. At lunch I head through a succession of narrow, zigzagging corridors to the nearest dining car, and join a table with three other diners. We talk about the state of politics in our countries, the latest books we've read, and where we're travelling to next as we watch the scenery roll gently by. The lunch selection includes a quiche with Caesar salad, stuffed green peppers, or – welcome to Canada – a bison burger. As I discover throughout my trip, food on board is generally very good, and the staff are unfailingly friendly and helpful.

Shortly after lunch we pass over French River. Three centuries ago, this shallow tributary of Georgian Bay, now designated a Canada Heritage River, was one of the waterways frequented by a group of explorers from Montreal. Known as *coureurs de bois* – the runners of the wood – these intrepid voyagers paddled canoes laden with goods to trade with the Amerindians in exchange for beaver pelts, venturing into the Great Lakes and deep into the vast uncharted land that lay beyond.

By mid-afternoon we are closing in on the city of Sudbury and the landscape begins to take on an increasingly eerie guise, with stunted, sparsely spaced trees. And there on the western horizon is the culprit: the 380-metre (1247-foot) smokestack of Inco company's nickel smelter. During the late 1960s, the Apollo astronauts bound for the moon came to Sudbury to train. In recent years, reforestation efforts and tighter pollution controls

ABOVE: *Colourful totem poles in Vancouver's Stanley Park, created by British Columbia's Haida First Nations to convey stories about their tribe.*

OPPOSITE: *The Canadian travels a route that was to be hacked through forests, laid over swamps and blasted through mountains.*

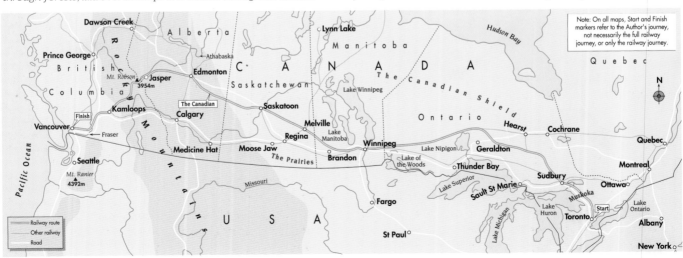

have helped but the area still looks a little like a man with a bad hair transplant – patchy in places.

North of the city, the train travels deeper and deeper into the Canadian Shield, a massive expanse of exposed Precambrian rock, some of the oldest on the planet, that extends all the way to the Arctic and as far west as the Rocky Mountains. This land of granite and gneiss dates back a billion years, and the intervening millennia have involved a complicated geological story of faulting, folding, and compression. But the current topography owes its biggest debt to the effects of glaciation over the last million years, as a succession of continental glaciers have scoured the ancient mountain range, scraping away the topsoil and creating countless depressions that have since filled in, creating one of the biggest collections of lakes and swamps on the planet. The vegetation is primarily boreal forest of spruce, pine, poplar, and larch, which blanket the land so thickly it is hard to imagine how the animal denizens such as moose and bear make their way through it. Not to mention the thousands of underpaid workers who were saddled with the task of laying rails along this route through a primeval land in the early 20th century. With picks and axes and blasting powder they punched holes through rock walls and slogged through mile after mile of boggy, boot-sucking ground known by the Ojibwa word *muskeg*. They weren't the first to breach the Shield with a ribbon of steel. In the early 1880s, builders of the Canadian Pacific Railway (CPR) line to Vancouver – Canada's first transcontinental line – wrestled with the same problem south of the path taken by the train today. CPR general manager William C. van Horne rated part of the stretch through the Shield as '320 kilometres (200 miles) of engineering hell.'

The area beyond Sudbury becomes increasingly desolate. I gaze out the window and a few 'stations' sail by – places like McFee's Camp, Felix, Ruel, and Mud River. Some are little more than a sprinkling of houses with a path that leads down to a nearby lake. The rare passengers who disembark at these isolated outposts are invariably trappers, fishermen or hunters, who head off into the trackless forest that seems to stretch, like Joseph Conrad's Thames in *The Heart of Darkness*, to the uttermost ends of the Earth. Canoeists also occasionally use these 'flagstops'; unloading their crafts from the baggage car near the front of the train and then paddling away into the wilderness, returning a few days or a few weeks later to be picked up by another train.

After dinner I head to the dome car nearest my cabin with my cup of tea. The moon has risen now and casts a dappled glow on the lakes that we pass. Ahead I can see 21 cars stretching in front of me, a 400-metre long (quarter-mile) behemoth, arcing this way and that as the train follows

ABOVE: *The various dining cars on* The Canadian *offer three sittings for lunch and dinner during summer and two sittings during the off-peak season.*

its circuitous route. The lights from the train illuminate a narrow swath beside the tracks, reflecting off the white birches. But the pine trees are mere dark forms etched against the inky blackness of the night sky. Above me, the pale glow of the Milky Way dominates the sky.

A quick nightcap at the bar in the rear car of the train and I return to my room. During dinner, the steward has folded down the bed from the wall, laid out the blankets and turned on my reading lamp. I sit propped up in bed with a magazine. After a few minutes, I turn off the light and look out through the window at the foot of my bed. Outside, the woods are, as poet Robert Frost put it, 'lovely, dark, and deep'. And when I awake several times during my restless night, I am greeted by the same view.

At breakfast I'm back at a table with my dinner companions from the previous night. While the waitress brings us our pancakes, sausages and morning coffee we chat and look out the windows on an even more awesome collection of lakes than the previous day. The woods here are home to large numbers of bear and moose, but whether it is the noise of the train or my less-than-flawless vision, I fail to see one. I do, however, spot

the telltale mark of beavers near the tracks – neatly gnawed trees that they will use to build the beaver lodges where they will spend the winter, well-insulated from the –40°C (–40°F) temperatures and the snow that will soon blanket the land.

A sign on the north side of the tracks announces that, after 1800 kilometres (1120 miles) and 30 hours on the rails, we have finally left the vast province of Ontario and entered Manitoba. Soon, the landscape changes. First it is the lakes and the rocky outcroppings – our constant companions for the past day – which begin to disappear. Then the track straightens out, stretching for miles without the slightest bend. Fields appear, some with rich, black earth. Slowly, miraculously, we emerge from the Canadian Shield into a world that becomes progressively flatter and flatter. The trees are also receding from view and by mid-afternoon we are travelling into the beginning of plains that extend west for hundreds of kilometres, through Saskatchewan, the neighbouring province, and into Alberta. Canadians know this land as the Prairies and it is among the most fertile patches in Canada – in the summer, a scene of endless fields of wheat. We cross a causeway and stop for an hour at Winnipeg, yet another Canadian city that owes its birth to the fur trade and the railway. Beyond the Manitoba capital, the flatness of the land is extraordinary, stretching off as far as the eye can see; only the occasional farm and grain elevators – tall storage silos – break the view. Locals call this 'big sky country' and it's true. The vaulting dome above us seems much vaster than anything I've ever seen in eastern Canada.

This being early November, night falls four hours earlier than in summer, so we are scarcely 50 kilometres (80 miles) beyond Winnipeg before darkness closes in. I opt for an early night and head to my bedroom. On the way I stop for a little post-dinner conversation in a dome car. One of the glories of train travel is the people you meet along the way. Maybe it's the type of traveller drawn to moving at a leisurely pace, rather than people who can't wait to get where they are going, but this trip introduces me to an interesting group. People like Keith, and his stories of surveying the Arctic regions of Canada; Don, the court reporter from Los Angeles, and his tales of the lesser deeds of Hollywood stars; Dutch, the retired conductor, and anecdotes from his years riding the rails through Canada. By the time this trip is over, I know I am going to miss some of them.

Back in my room I observe that the ever-changing Prairie weather has dumped 15 centimetres (6 inches) of snow just

inside the Saskatchewan border. I shut off the lights and peer outside. Few things are cozier than lying under the blankets in a train bed and watching a snowbound landscape flashing by a few feet away. I feel wonderfully snug and happy. The sky has cleared and the stars are out in force, as well as some strange lights that flash up into the sky all along the northern horizon: *Aurora Borealis*, the northern lights. I am mesmerized by it and though part of me feels like nodding off to sleep, I continue to watch the celestial display as the train thunders along through the night on its northwesterly arc through Saskatchewan. Sleep proves less fitful on my second night on the train. Gary, the barman, tells me that the first night is the hardest, the second night easier, and by the third night the porters have trouble waking you up. By the time I get up we have sailed clear through the rest of Saskatchewan

and the snow and entered Alberta, with a new landscape of rolling hills. This is one of the appeals of rail travel: the speed is slow enough to have you constantly wondering what lies just around the next bend and yet fast enough to present a continually changing panorama.

Just after sunrise, the train pulls into Edmonton for a one-hour service stop. No time to head out to the West Edmonton

---

ABOVE: *A freight train with hopper cars full of wheat from the Canadian Prairies leaves Jasper, Alberta. After travelling through the Rocky Mountains into British Columbia, the train will dislodge its cargo at the port city of Vancouver. The railway in Canada has long played a central role in transporting both people and goods across the great expanses of the country.*

Mall, the world's largest mall, with 800 stores, a skating rink, an amusement park and a tank that offers submarine rides. But that's fine. I'm itching for the train to leave because the next leg will take us to the Rocky Mountains.

Unfortunately, the weather isn't co-operating. We're back in snow country. On a clear day you can usually spot the Rockies from near the town of Edson but we are 100 kilometres (62 miles) beyond that point today and still have no inkling that we are nearing their presence as the falling snow confines visibility to a less than a 100 metres. Eventually, the snow lets up and I begin to make out the mountains, their snow-covered form disappearing seamlessly into a leaden-grey sky. We follow the shores of the Athabaska River into Jasper, passing a group of four elk along the way.

We reach Jasper at 14:00 and stop for an hour. The town is dominated by shops and restaurants catering to the tourist trade, and after a quick tour I hop back on the train and

we set off. Soon we are climbing, snaking our way through the mountains and heading toward Yellowhead Pass. The weather conditions are changing almost upon the instant with fog that drifts by and clouds that scud across the landscape. One moment I am looking at a mountain peak; a minute later and it is no longer there and I wonder whether I ever saw it in the first place. By now, it is standing-room only in the rear dome-observation car. We follow the shore of Moose Lake. Its bluish-green waters provide a sombre double image of mountain peaks that fade away into the fog and clouds. Soon we cross Yellowhead Pass on the Continental Divide, the point from which all waters flow

ABOVE: *Canada's third-largest city, Vancouver, is beautifully situated on the shores of the Pacific Ocean in British Columbia. It was named after Captain George Vancouver, who was the first European to discover the area in 1792.*

either west to the Pacific, north to the Arctic Ocean, or east to the Atlantic. This also marks our entry into the last of the five provinces on our journey, British Columbia. All eyes are peeled for Mount Robson – at 3954 metres (12,970 feet) the highest peak in the Canadian Rockies. We think we spot it several times but no one is sure. Ahead, the sky has begun to clear on the horizon and the setting sun begins to peek through. Half an hour ago I did not think that we would see blue sky before nightfall. But now, a small patch opens up. Someone calls out, 'There's Robson!' I turn around expecting to see a peak slightly higher than the others. But no – this mountain towers above the rest, a mammoth snow-covered form that stretches impossibly high into the sky. The timing is perfect. The dying rays of sunlight shine on Robson, bathing it briefly in a rosy hue, as though the sun has singled it out from the rest of the mountains that cluster around it. Many of the people in the car have travelled far and wide in the world but all are rendered speechless. Someone starts

clapping and the whole car erupts with applause. I think of the Romantic poets of the early 19th century and their concept of the sublime – something that quite literally takes your breath away. For a few moments this day, I have experienced the sublime.

I sleep well that night – Gary was right. Arriving at the dining car at 06:30 the next day, I eat a quick meal of porridge and head back to my room. The train is scheduled to arrive in Vancouver in an hour. I pack my bag and sit and watch out of my window as we hug the shores of the muddy, salmon-rich waters of the Fraser River snaking its way into Vancouver. Many visitors to Canada rate this city as their favourite destination; and with good reason. Situated on the Pacific Ocean and rimmed by an impressive backdrop of mountain peaks, it is one of North America's most beautifully located cities – and a fitting end to my journey. I take a last look around at my home for the previous three days, and head outside into the fresh morning air.

The Coast Starlight

LOS ANGELES TO SEATTLE

by Tom Savio

THE COAST STAR-LIGHT IS AMTRAK'S THOROUGHBRED train. It threads a 2235-kilo-metre (1389-mile) path along the surf and across the mountains linking the history, landscape and unique characters of California, Oregon and Washington. Like all thoroughbreds, the *Starlight* has a pedigree – the Southern Pacific Company's *Coast Daylight* that served Los Angeles and San Francisco. The *Daylight* was created during the doldrums of the Great Depression to lure Californians back to the rails. The scarlet and orange streamliner reflected the Western sunsets and promise of brighter days to come. The *Daylight* became part of California folklore and America's most popular train, distinctions Amtrak's *Coast Starlight* continues to claim today.

In the 1990s Amtrak, the government entity that operates America's intercity passenger trains over the freight railroads, chartered a new course to attract patronage with innovative services while decreasing its dependence on subsidies. The task of recasting the *Coast Starlight* fell to Amtrak's rail visionaries Gil Mallery and Brian Rosenwald. It was a radical plan, but on America's 'Left Coast', where rebellion in the arts, politics and technology is de rigueur, it worked.

Most of the passenger cars Amtrak had inherited from the private railroads were, by that time, fodder for the scrap furnaces. However, the stainless steel carriages built by the Budd Company have legendary longevity; one test engineer suggested that they were the first 'permanent structures' ever built. So when Mallery and Rosenwald spotted the cream of the Budd Co's workshops – the glass-domed, double-deck lounges from the Santa Fe *El Capitan* – on a derelict siding, they rescued the classics. The cars were refurbished with hardwood bars, swivel seats, hot *hors d'oeuvres* tables and video theatres, then dubbed the *Pacific Parlour Cars* (using the regal British spelling). These railway penthouses, reserved for sleeping car guests, set the tone for the new *Coast Starlight*. Despite its swank amenities, the *Starlight* is still a working train – hauling cut flowers and express parcels in its baggage car – while carrying travellers to college towns, holiday resorts and cosmopolitan cities.

My *Starlight* journey began from LA's magnificent marble and tile Union Station. The tract of land it occupies was once home to the Chinese who came to California to build its railways. When the railroads redeveloped the land in 1939 and erected the Los Angeles Union Passenger Terminal, they created one of the finest civic buildings in the West.

We left the Los Angeles Basin through the Santa Susanna Pass earthquake zone, which is part of a system of faults that bisects California for hundreds of miles and lurks deep and uncomfortably in its psyche. Near Ventura we encountered the Pacific Ocean, which became our travelling companion for the next 182 kilometres (113 miles). The surfers, sunbathers, willowy eucalyptus trees and lush citrus groves so prevalent along the coast recalled an older, genteel California – a lost paradise that is still reflected in the *Starlight's*

ABOVE: *Steward trainee Josue Martinez meticulously sets the tables onboard the exclusive* Pacific Parlour Car.
RIGHT: *Los Angeles' Union Station, a Spanish Revival tour de force, was the last great railway terminal built in America and is perhaps the most beautiful.*

windows. Lunch was served in the dining car while the train skimmed along the cliffs and crossed high trestles perched above the breakers. At mid-afternoon, vintages from some of California's leading vineyards were sampled during the customary wine tasting in the parlour car.

Leaving the ocean behind at San Luis Obispo, the *Starlight* clawed its way up 300 metres (980 feet) over Cuesta Grade and the Santa Lucia Mountains in a dramatic procession of curves and tunnels. Throughout the day, we passed farms, vineyards and cattle ranches – agriculture is California's biggest business. The train paused in Salinas, 'the nation's salad bowl', near the National Steinbeck Center. The American novelist John Steinbeck grew up in Salinas and chronicled the darker side of California agriculture. His hometown disowned him, but a recent downturn in its 'ag' fortunes persuaded it to cultivate tourists with the long-overdue museum.

Further north in the San Francisco Bay Area, the *Starlight* picked its way past the docks of Oakland, calling at Jack London Square Station. Here, 80 years before 'brewpubs', the yarn spinner frequented the First and Last Chance Saloon – a rustic bar that still serves up cool ones to thirsty sailors and stevedores. San Francisco-bound passengers board buses here for the ride over the Bay Bridge to the city baptized 'Baghdad by the Bay' by celebrated local columnist Herb Caen.

We flashed past 'Berzerkley', flagship campus of the University of California and ground zero of the counter-culture. In 1964 my brother Mario declared 'Free Speech' from the roof of a police car there and was booted from the university for 'committing history without a license'. Thirty years later he was memorialized with a bronze plaque on the school's front steps. As night closed in, I drew the curtains shut around my berth and dozed away the miles and family memories. The *Starlight* continued to Sacramento, the state capital, a provincial town that inexplicably governs the world's sixth largest economy. Near the station, the first earth was turned for the Transcontinental Railroad. When the line to the East was completed in 1869, the promises, riches, legends and opportunities of

ABOVE: *The* Coast Starlight *near San Luis Obispo, shortly after leaving the Pacific coast to climb towards the Cuesta Grade, en route to San Francisco.*

the 'Golden State' were thrown open to any individual who could afford a ticket as cheap as US$1. It was the ultimate expression of American democracy.

We were running very late, although not unexpectedly, since crusty railroaders call our train the *Starlate*. However, it had an unexpected benefit: I awoke to see Mount Shasta's towering peak (4267 metres; 14,000 feet) from my compartment window, a sight usually cloaked by night.

California's dry and tawny 'golden' hills gave way to Oregon's lakes and waterfalls, framed in ferns and shaded by evergreens. We passed the morning zigzagging over the Cascades. When the *Starlight* passed the Weyerhaeuser paper mill near the Mohawk Valley, I recalled the last

days of the *Mohawk Rocket* log train. Its ambling rails were bordered with wild apple trees. For generations, lumberjacks riding its buggies snacked on apples and threw the cores of the fruit along the line, giving rise to the trees as well as to an Oregon legend. After leaving Portland's rambling pile-of-bricks station, we crossed the broad Columbia River into Washington State. Unwinding from its headwaters far in the Canadian Rockies like a cornucopia, the Columbia River nourishes the wheat fields, orchards and salmon that are the hallmarks of the Pacific Northwest.

The first sign that we were arriving in Seattle's King Street Station was the menacing glance of the ubiquitous Starbucks coffee girl, glowing from her billboard tower. I must be the only person in America who has second thoughts about this nerdy, mid-American San Francisco. However, come the morning I woke up to ferry boats, totem poles and the Space Needle that are set around a splendid harbour nestling beneath the glaciers of Mount Rainier.

ABOVE: *The Starlight runs alongside the Pacific Ocean surf for 182 kilometres (113 miles), pulled by two GE Genesis Class DASH9-P42B diesel electrics.*

Denver & Rio Grande Railway

DURANGO & SILVERTON NARROW GAUGE RAILROAD
CUMBRES & TOLTEC SCENIC RAILROAD

by Steve Barry

IN THE LATE 1880s, THE ROCKY Mountains of Colorado were full of untapped resources, including silver. The rough, athough magnificent, terrain provided a formidable obstacle to the railroad builders wanting to access these resources.

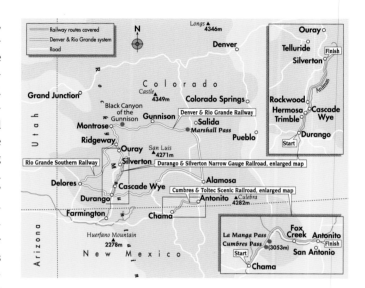

Their solution was to run 'narrow gauge' tracks into the mountains – only 0.9 metres (3 feet) between the rails – instead of 'standard gauge' of 1.478 metres (4 feet 8½ inches). The Denver & Rio Grande Railway started at Ouray, went north to Montrose, east to Mears Junction via Marshall Pass, south to Alamosa, west to Durango and north to Silverton. Ouray and Silverton were separated by 830 kilometres (515 miles) of track, but only 24 kilometres (15 miles) as the crow flies.

The Rio Grande Southern, completed in 1891, ran from the Denver & Rio Grande at Durango, headed northwest to Dolores and north to Ridgeway, rejoining the Denver & Rio Grande just north of Ouray and completing a 'narrow gauge circle' around southwest Colorado. In later years, the incursion of standard gauge tracks into narrow gauge territory began to take its toll, but the narrow gauge lines survived for a time. The prosperity of silver had been replaced by more stable commodities of lumber, livestock and coal, keeping the lines running for 50 years.

In 1949, the first break in the circle occurred when the tracks were torn up through the Black Canyon of the Gunnison as increased rail traffic moved over the standard gauge railroads. Over the next six years, the circle was reduced to shambles, and by 1955 only the tracks between

Alamosa and Durango remained, along with branch line tracks north and south out of Durango to Silverton and Farmington, New Mexico. By 1967, only the Silverton branch from Durango, which had been discovered by tourists, was still in operation. Two pieces of the narrow gauge empire remain. The Silverton branch from Durango is now operated as the Durango & Silverton Narrow Gauge Railroad. And in 1970 the states of Colorado and New Mexico bought the only remaining segment of the circle, 72 kilometres (45 miles) of

ABOVE: *A southbound Durango & Silverton train clings to the rock shelf on the 'high line' north of Rockwood, with the Animas River rushing far below.*

OPPOSITE: *A pair of 2-8-2 'Mikado' steam locomotives power a Cumbres & Toltec Scenic train through Los Pinos, en route to Cumbres Pass.*

track between Antonito, Colorado, and Chama, New Mexico. This is now operated as the Cumbres & Toltec Scenic Railroad. The railroads are similar, in that they both feature narrow gauge tracks traversing flatlands and mountains and both feature steam locomotives that originally ran for the succes-

sor, Denver & Rio Grande Western. Despite their similarities, however, there are dramatic differences as well. The Durango & Silverton has become a 'glitzy' affair, as both of its namesake towns have become tourist meccas, whereas the Cumbres & Toltec has retained much of its original character.

Durango & Silverton Narrow Gauge Railroad

DURANGO TO SILVERTON

THE DURANGO & SILVERTON NARROW GAUGE Railroad is tucked away in the southwest corner of the state of Colorado, a seven hour drive from Denver, the nearest major city. Yet the railway draws more than 250,000 passengers a year to ride its steam-powered narrow gauge trains. The history of the Durango & Silverton line can be traced back to the 1880s when the 'narrow gauge circle' was being built around southwest Colorado. The area around Silverton had vast deposits of silver in the Rocky Mountains surrounding the town, and the railroad company was eager to tap the mines. They built a line northward from Durango on the narrow gauge circle, along the Animas River to Silverton. After the silver mines ran dry, the branch was used to haul other resources from the mountains.

Just about the time the Silverton branch had outlived its usefulness, tourists discovered the line and came flocking to view its scenic treasures. While the main line of the narrow gauge circle was being abandoned, the Silverton branch soldiered on, still connected to the outside world by the last thread of narrow gauge tracks between Durango and Alamosa. The Denver & Rio Grande Western (successor to the Denver & Rio Grande) expanded operations on the Silverton branch, but much of the line's historic integrity was sacrificed. Fake diamond smokestacks were attached to the steam locomotives and many of the original structures and trackwork in the Durango yard were demolished. The popularity of the Silverton branch continued to grow, but ultimately the all-freight (and all standard gauge) Denver & Rio Grande

Western decided to get out of the passenger business. In 1982, just after the 100th anniversary of the branch, the line was sold to Florida businessman Charles Bradshaw. Railroad buffs rejoiced when the first thing Bradshaw did was remove the fake diamond stacks and restore the locomotives to their original appearance.

The popularity of the Silverton branch today has turned it into a year-round attraction. During the peak tourist months, four complete trains with up to 10 coaches, leave Durango for the all-day run to Silverton and most are sold out in advance. The winter trains only travel as far north as Cascade Wye, about a third of the way to Silverton, but the snow-covered mountains and forests are well worth seeing. Durango itself is a surprisingly busy town, and it owes its prosperity to the narrow-gauge railroad. To get into the mood for a trip back in

RIGHT: *The Durango & Silverton Narrow Gauge train steams along the banks of the Animas River, with the Rockies towering above, on the run to Silverton.*

time aboard an authentic steam engine, book a room at the traditional Strater Hotel just a block from the station.

A day riding the Silverton begins with picking up your tickets at the original Durango station early in the morning. Car assignments may be either a coach (rather small due to the size restrictions of narrow gauge railroading) or an open-air car built from an old freight car, both at the same fare. The deluxe extra fare Silver Vista dome car is also available on some runs. The coaches are all 'open window' – no air-conditioning on this railroad (not that you need it in the cool Rocky Mountain air). These are not luxury accommodations, but rather the same style of coach used when the line was built in 1881, all of which contributes to the ambience of the ride.

Departing Durango, the first hour of the trip is spent almost directly on the shoulder of US Highway 550. When the train stops at the Hermosa tank to take on water, close inspection reveals that the big yellow wooden tank is merely decorative and that water is actually drawn from a more modern steel tank nearby. The railroad next enters San Juan National Forest. The forest is filled with evergreens, so winter is particularly beautiful – towering 'Christmas trees' blanketed in snow line both sides of the track. The railroad leaves the flat valley north of Durango and penetrates the mountains through a narrow pass up to Rockwood, the last place the line is within sight of a road until Silverton. After passing a small railway maintenance yard, the train punches through Rockwood Cut, where the rocks are scant inches from the side of the coaches.

The Animas River (Spanish for River of Lost Souls) appears below the tracks and the steam locomotives work hard as the track climbs above it. Suddenly the train pops out onto a narrow ledge, where the rail ties (sleepers) are mere inches from a sheer cliff. Looking down, passengers once again catch sight of the raging river more than 300 metres (1000 feet) below. The 'high line' lasts only a few minutes, ending as the train crosses the river, but it is the most breathtaking part of the trip.

Soon the tracks and the river are nearly on the same level again, the Animas remaining visible for the remainder of the trip into Silverton. From the exclusive vacation resort of Tall Timbers, accessible only by train or helicopter, the rest of the ride is through rugged countryside. The peaks of the Rockies, snow-covered for much of the year, tower over you as the train crawls along the canyon floor, ultimately popping out of

ABOVE: *K28 Class locomotive No. 476 steams into the station with one of the four daily trains that traverse the Durango & Silverton Narrow Gauge Railway.*

Cumbres & Toltec Scenic Railroad

CHAMA TO ANTONITO

WORKING OUT OF CHAMA, NEW MEXICO, the Cumbres & Toltec Scenic Railroad runs over the sole remaining 103 kilometres (64 miles) of the once 830-kilometre (515-mile) Denver & Rio Grande 'narrow gauge circle'. For the best experience, ride the line in its entirety from Chama, a quiet New Mexico town that remains virtually unchanged since the 1950s, to Antonito in Colorado.

Your day can start well before the train departs, as Chama has an authentic rail yard that has retained much of its mid-20th century character. At the engine house it is possible to observe the locomotives being prepared for the day's journey, and photographers will find many opportunities to capture steam shooting from the iron beasts into the cool Rocky Mountain air.

Two – sometimes three – locomotives are attached to the front of the train for the tortuous climb from Chama (2693 metres; 7863 feet) to the summit at Cumbres Pass (3053 metres; 10,015 feet). The locomotives are all of the same 2-8-2 wheel arrangement, known as a Mikado type. Locomotive No. 463, the smallest engine on the line, once belonged to cowboy movie star Gene Autry. Converted from railroad boxcars, passenger coaches are spartan and have open windows.

For the best vistas, find a seat on the right side of the train. With two blasts of the whistle, the train sets off. Soon after crossing the Chama River there appears to be a town straight out of an old Western, right in the middle of a meadow. Known as 'Lobato', a name it shares with a nearby bridge, this town was constructed as a movie set some years ago and today

stands abandoned, closed to the public. Just beyond the town lies Lobato Trestle, the first of several high steel bridges on the line. As the train crosses this mountain stream fed by melting snow, meadows and evergreen forests give way to rocky terrain devoid of vegetation, and the noise from the locomotives becomes increasingly louder as the train starts to dig into a four per cent grade (1 unit of elevation per 4 units of distance). For rail fans, this is without doubt the best part of the trip – there is nothing like the magnificent display of a steam locomotive working its heart out on a grade.

Part way through the climb, the locomotives have used enough water to require a stop at the Cresco water tank. Out of Cresco, the train swings across Colorado Route 17 making the final steep climb over Windy Point. The train comes to a stop at Cumbres Pass, for a vertiginous view down to the valley

RIGHT: *One of several 2-8-2 narrow-gauge locomotives used on the Cumbres & Toltec Scenic crests the summit of Cumbres Pass, at an altitude of more than 3053 metres (10,015 feet).*

floor below. It is all downhill from here and one of the two locomotives required to make the climb out of Chama will be left behind at Cumbres. Dropping down from Cumbres, the train twists back on itself through the famous Tanglefoot Curve, and meets up with Route 17 again as it passes a row of new homes built along the roadside. Water is replenished at the Los Pinos tank and for the next 80 kilometres (50 miles) it is entirely possible you won't see another human being until Osier.

Between Los Pinos and Osier the train leaves the valley floor and clings to the walls of the gorge. Hugging the mountain, it slowly works its way back down towards the green valley floor and soon crosses Cascade Trestle, one of the more spectacular bridges on the line. Looking down, the bridge itself is obscured and it appears as if the train is literally hanging, suspended over the rocky creek bed hundreds of feet below. A few kilometres later, a hot meal awaits your lunchtime arrival at Osier, where the train from Chama meets the train from Antonito.

Here the locomotives from the two trains will swap passenger cars. As a result, the cars that came from Chama and Antonito will return to their starting points. The locomotives, however, will continue operating in the same direction they were heading, eliminating the need to turn them.

A few miles east of Osier, the Antonito train goes through Rock Tunnel and bursts out into the spectacular Toltec Gorge. Clinging to the mountain, the track winds its way along many unusual rock formations, at one point curving through a series of rock spires known as Phantom Curve; it was here that a snowslide carried a passenger train over the side in 1948. In autumn, the hillsides are ablaze with golden leaves as the aspen trees change colour. Mud Tunnel is the second (and last) tunnel the train goes through, and a few miles further on the locomotive is treated to a drink of water at the tiny settlement of Sublette.

The last leg of the trip takes travellers from Chama through scenery far different to that which they have encountered up to this point. The track starts to wind down the hills outside Antonito, and trees slowly give way to wide open sage lands. Soon the town appears in the distance. Even though it is only about 10 kilometres (6 miles) to town as the crow flies, the track curves gently down the face of the hills, twisting back on itself three times at Whiplash Curve, and covering a total of 20 kilometres (12 miles) before reaching Antonito.

ABOVE: *Minutes out of Chama, New Mexico, a Cumbres & Toltec Scenic train passes through the meadow at Lobato.*

The Copper Canyon Railway

EL FUERTE TO CHIHUAHUA

by Philip Game

DEEP INSIDE THE SIERRA MADRE OF northwestern Mexico, the green-walled Barrancas del Cobre, or copper canyons, tumble to greater depths than Arizona's Grand Canyon. Rich lodes of gold and silver, not copper, awaited the Spaniards who packed their bullion out along *El Camino Real*, the royal road which still serves as a bridle path three centuries later. This rugged terrain is traversed by one of the world's most dramatic train rides. In just 653 kilometres (406 miles) the railway crosses 39 bridges and penetrates 87 tunnels as it climbs to more than 2400 metres (7800 feet) from the steamy tropical plains of the state of Sinaloa, through canyons, up to the pine-covered mountains of the Sierra Tarahumara and onto the high, rolling wheatfields of the Altiplano.

The *Chihuahua al Pacífico*, known locally as *El Chepe*, opened in 1961, a century after the American engineer and religious visionary Albert Kinsey Owens began his campaign to link the American Midwest with the Pacific coast and Asia. By late 1999 Mexico's former state-owned railway no longer operated passenger trains on the trunk routes south of the United States border. As I rode by bus down the Pacific coast, I caught one glimpse of the parlous state of the Mexican railroads: at Empalme, outside Guaymas, empty carriages and freight wagons stood, for mile after mile, rusting along the disused sidings. Ferrocarril Mexicano was created following privatisation of the national railway in February 1998. Today, Ferromex operates the 12-hour ride between Los Mochis, a city on Mexico's Pacific coast facing the Baja California peninsula, and the inland metropolis of Chihuahua (due south of El Paso, Texas), where services now terminate. On this route, it is the section from El Fuerte to Creel, high in the Sierra, which encompasses the highlights. Passengers travelling along this stretch enjoy the full impact of three magnificent canyons, Septentrion, Urique and Tararecua, with distant views of a fourth, Barranca del Cobre, the copper canyon that lends its name to the region.

There are also glimpses of the indigenous Tarahumara, a colourful if taciturn people. They call themselves the Raramuri, 'foot runners', an apt designation as they are famed for their ability to run for days without rest, while hunting deer. During Semana Santa, the Easter Holy Week festival, the Tarahumara perform dances and ritual jousts which interweave their tribal beliefs with the Catholic convention introduced by 17th-century Jesuits.

Aside from Semana Santa, the best time to visit Mexico's Sierra Madre is early autumn. In a good year, the canyons are clothed in velvet green, with the mists that rise up each morning returning as the afternoon deluge. Tortuous roads descend into the tropical depths of each canyon; the six-hour trip which switchbacks 2000 metres (6562 feet) from Creel down to the old mining town of Batopilas has to be one of the Third World's epic bus journeys.

The bus ride inland from Los Mochis demonstrates why most travellers pass up the first leg of the *Chihuahua Al*

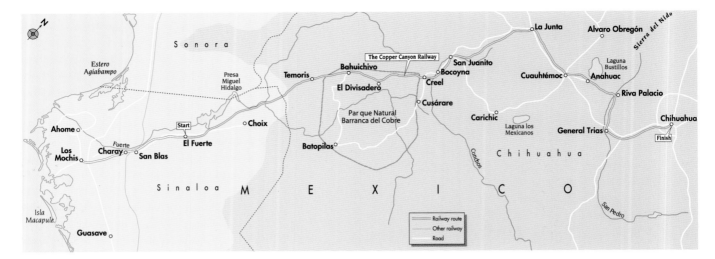

Pacífico. It is a dead-straight 80-kilometre (48-mile) ride across dusty farmlands, and the time is better spent exploring El Fuerte, a colonial garrison founded by the *conquistadores* in 1564. El Fuerte's Posada del Hidalgo is reminiscent of the *Paradors*, those great inns of the Iberian Peninsula. Inside the pastel-toned walls, shady colonnades and courtyard gardens set off such treasures as a family-owned horse-drawn hearse. At the establishment's 'Curious Shop' I purchased my ticket on the next day's first-class train.

It is six in the morning in El Fuerte. Lights soon switch on over the plywood stands set up on the cobbled streets: coffee, hot chocolate and savoury *taquitos* coming up. At the station outside town, North American tour groups, self-sufficient enthusiasts and sinewy backpackers mill about the open-air platform. When the train does pull in, it is close on eight o' clock. Facilities on board are exemplary, although catering proves slow. Four off-duty crew select, receive and demolish a hearty breakfast of ham, eggs and coffee before my modest order materializes. Several purposeful, solidly-built men wearing pistol holsters and pressed trousers provide a security escort; the atmosphere, however, remains relaxed.

The first-class *Primera Express* operates four 68-passenger carriages, plus a dining car for 41 passengers and a lounge

LEFT: *The* Chihuahua al Pacífico *climbing into the mountains near Témoris.*
OPPOSITE TOP: *A torrid afternoon in the 16th-century colonial garrison town of El Fuerte, where the train begins its climb into the Sierra Tarahumara.*
OPPOSITE BOTTOM: *Tarahumara Indians relaxing in Batopilas.*

smoking bar car. The refurbished cars have been fitted with carpets and reclining chairs, heaters and air-conditioning and washrooms with proper waste disposal. The Economy Class train, once grimy and uncomfortable, has been greatly improved through the installation of air-conditioners and heaters in every car, new rest rooms, new seats, a new snack bar and a wagon for small freight (of great benefit to cyclists).

In late morning the train enters the mountains at Témoris, where three levels of track meet to negotiate the canyon formed by the Rio Septentrion. On the river flats, fields of Indian corn surround dusty cottages built of adobe and corrugated iron. Here the track curves across two bridges to reverse its direction, and then ascends a series of loops before disappearing into a long tunnel. By midday we have inched past hillsides of *piñon* pine, live oak and juniper and up onto a stony plateau lightly forested with ponderosa pine and Douglas fir. At Posada Barrancas station, the apricot-coloured cabins of the luxurious Posada Mirador perch at 2200 metres (7220 feet) above sea level, right on the rim of the canyon. Ten minutes further on the canyon-rim station at Divisadero, a halt for sightseeing, is crowded with vendors of *burritos*, postcards and handcrafts. By late afternoon the locomotive is clattering into Creel, which is a rough-edged lumber town on the flank of an *arroyo*, or steep-sided, dry valley. Souvenir stores rub shoulders with one-room general stores (boots, canned food, stetson hats) and pseudo-alpine tourist guest-houses, as cottonwood trees glow in the sinking sun.

From Creel, a journey of five-and-a-half hours brings you to the terminus at Chihuahua. After the Sierra Madre and the high, rolling wheat fields of the Altiplano, the city seems enormous, a glittering oasis of bright lights, smart cars and stylish women. Six-lane boulevards run for miles past supermarkets and used-car dealers, while the stately town centre harks back to the Victorian era. This is big-sky country, an arid land of cattle ranches, haciendas and high desert plains. Chihuahua State covers a territory the size of France and neither city nor state admits to any connection with a certain breed of diminutive dogs. It takes me a while to match the pace of this place; beyond noon, the streets are sparsely populated, the light harsh. Somewhere around 16:30, the heat fades and people begin to reappear as the hole-in-the-wall stores reopen, and the market district begins to bustle.

On Calle Victoria, a couple of blocks from the prostitutes in Calle 10a, affluent young women unwind at *Café de los*

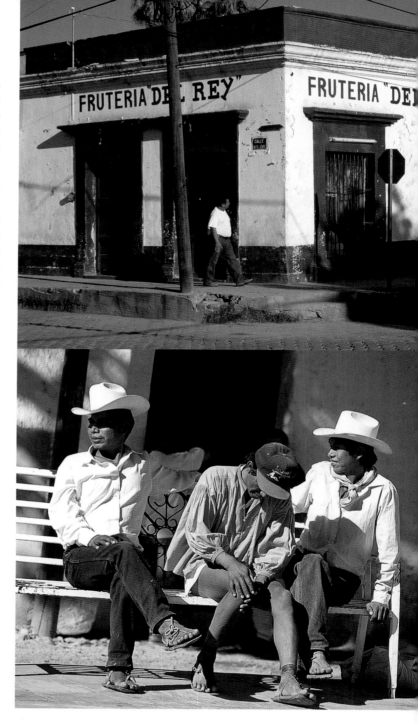

Milagros, making for a scene as sophisticated as that to be found in any major city: designer cocktails, exotic coffees and gourmet grazing in an eggshell-blue historic villa. *El Chepe* has transported me through Mexico on many levels: from the tar-paper grunge of tiny Tarahumara hamlets to the bright lights of Chihuahua.

The Puno–Cusco Line

PUNO TO CUSCO

by Graham Simmons

AT 4780 METRES (15,690 FEET) ABOVE sea level Peru's Galera station on the Lima–Huancayo line is said to be the highest standard gauge railway station in the Americas, but sadly, until very recently the line was only open to freight traffic. La Raya, the highest station accessible to passenger trains is, however, also in Peru, on the Puno–Cusco line.

Railways in Peru have a proud history. In the middle of the 1800s South America was being opened up to enterprise driven by European and North American capital. Resources in Peru and Bolivia waiting to be plundered included the enormous mineral deposits of the Andes, and rubber from the Amazon forests. Accordingly, railways were built to link the major cities of Peru and Bolivia. The resulting network is one of the world's greatest feats of railway engineering, crossing almost impregnable mountain country.

The Puno–Cusco line was a later addition to Peru's railway system. It was built by the British in 1907 partly to service the alpaca wool trade. At more than 3800 metres (12,400 feet) above sea level, Puno is a picturesque town set on the shores of Lake Titicaca, which is the world's highest navigable lake.

ABOVE: *Disconsolate passengers await developments near their broken down train in southern Peru.*
LEFT: *The Puno–Cusco train near Blanca, in central Peru. It is powered by a Model 352 diesel locomotive which takes 10 hours to haul the train along the mountainous 408-kilometre (254-mile) route.*

A sign outside the regional hospital offers 'Psychosomatic Examination for Driver's Licence', and judging by the antics of the kamikaze truck drivers who dominate the roads around these parts, it may well be far safer to travel by rail.

The train from Puno to Cusco leaves at 08:00. It was once a struggle just to get on it as a swarm of vendors vied for tourist dollars, and once aboard, travellers could expect to be robbed if they left their belongings for just a second. PeruRail (the new concession shared by James Sherwood's Orient-Express group and Peruvian Trains & Railways) saw the need to counter negative perceptions and an even more negative reality, and in a colossal and sustained effort, the railway has stationed security officials to guard the station entrance, preventing vendors and other non-travellers from boarding the train. As a result, rail aficionados can enjoy this great journey without paranoia.

Currently, there are two levels of service on the Puno–Cusco route: the Backpaper (economy class), which is popular among locals and treckers, and the deluxe American Explorer with gourmet meals and an observation car.

While my journey came with no insurance against a bumpy ride over the unwelded rail joints, after PeruRail took over the track was vastly improved and the former 'oval' wheels were made round. The stupendous scenery along the rail line is ample compensation for any temporary discomfort. As the train trundles out of the station for the long, 10-hour haul northwards, it soon becomes clear that we will be treated to a visual feast without parallel.

The Puno–Cusco line is the stuff of legend. Before the railway cleaned up its act, there were stories of delays well beyond the tolerable, with late-night arrivals and long waits in freezing, unlit carriages being par for the course. One of my fellow passengers recounted how on one occasion the

train was delayed for 75 minutes in Juliaca while the driver looked for oil at the right price. The engines also gave cause for concern – trains pulled along by locomotives of various shapes and sizes would often swap when they met halfway. Today, however, the locomotives are reliable diesels and passengers can usually be assured of punctuality.

The Puno–Cusco railway seamlessly joins two distinct halves of Peru – the Aymara-speaking south and the Quechua-speaking north. The empire of the Aymara originated on the Bolivian shores of Lake Titicaca. According to the Aymara, the world was created by the great god Viracocha, who arose from the lake and created all human beings, the sun, moon and the stars, the movement of which created Time itself. The Inca on the other hand are descended from the Quechua ethnic group. The founders of the Inca empire, a semi-mythical figure known as Manco Capac and his sister-wife Mama Ocllo, are said to have led their tribe on a trek, under supernatural guidance, to a mountaintop stronghold that later became the city of Cusco. While the Incas share with the Aymara a belief in the creator god Viracocha, the official religion under the Inca conquerors in the 1400s became sun worship, with the emperor and his clan of nobles being referred to as 'Children of the Sun'.

The track north from Puno passes along what is called the *Corredor Quechua*, which leads from Puno, in the Aymara

region, to Cusco, the heart of Quechua culture. The first stop is at Sillustani, railhead for the famous *chullpas*, which are cylindrical monuments guarding the tombs of the Hatumcolla chiefs who once ruled the area. Leaders were buried here along with their entire families, in tombs constructed with their openings facing east. It was believed that as the sun rose and penetrated a tomb, the family would be reborn.

Pukara, which is just more than 100 kilometres (60 miles) north of Puno, is famous for the production of pottery bulls, which the locals sell along the tracks. Until the arrival of the Spaniards in 1600 the bull was an unknown animal in Peru, but today these figures decorate the roofs of every house in the area.

The busy town of Juliaca, just 50 metres (164 feet) lower than Puno, is a rail junction for freight trains coming

from the south (Puno) and southwest (Arequipa). Just 20 kilometres (12 miles) further northwest, we pass through the 'Pink City' of Lampa, a pretty little town with a superb church, *La Immaculada*, which is said to house a copy of Michelangelo's *Pietà*.

The small town of Chuquibanbilla, a little further along the rail route, is the site of the new Altiplano Technological University. The university is pioneering some bold new experimental trials, cross-breeding llamas and alpacas; the idea is to produce a wool that combines the fineness of alpaca wool with the durability of llama wool. In addition, the meat of such a cross-breed will be tastier and more tender than llama meat (an important food source for Quechua and Aymara alike). At Ayaviri I buy a skewer of the regional speciality, Ayaviri mutton, from one of the many vendors who

approach the window of the train. One taste of the unpalatable meat and it becomes apparent why Ayaviri mutton is strictly a regional delicacy.

Nearly 40 kilometres (25 miles) north of Ayaviri, at 4000 metres (13,100 feet) above sea level, lies the town of Santa Rosa, famous for its fighting bulls. Towering more than 5000 metres (16,500 feet) above the town are the twin peaks of Kunurana and Chinmoya. Kunurana Glacier, known as 'the glacier with eternal snow', is located in the northwest cordillera of

ABOVE: *Narrow iron railway bridges spanning swift mountain torrents are common in the dramatic, rocky terrain of the Central Cordillera. The rugged beauty of the landscape is ample compensation for the discomfort of the bumpy ride along the unwelded rails of this line.*

Sicuani, at 3960 metres (12,993 feet), was for many years the terminus of the railway line. It is known as the 'traditional land of poets and writers', and in such idyllic surroundings it would not be difficult to find inspiration. Sadly, the only recent author whose work I was able to authenticate is Fanni Muñoz Cabrejo, who in 1999 published a work entitled *The 'Flight' of the Dragon: the Culture of Opium in Lima in the '90s*. Sicuani is also an important market town, and a great place to shop for traditional crafts such as caps and rugs made from alpaca wool. An excellent craft market is held here on Sunday mornings.

About 25 kilometres (16 miles) northwest of Sicuani, the village of Raqchi (near San Pedro) is the site for one of Peru's biggest folkloric festivals, which is held each year in mid-June. Dominating the landscape and clearly visible from the train are the ruins of the great Temple of Viracocha, which was dedicated to the god credited with the creation of the universe, sacred not only to the Aymara but also to the Inca.

Another 15 kilometres (9 miles) further lies the village of Tinta, the birthplace of the Tupac Umaru guerrilla movement, widely accused of the attempted destruction (not the creation) of the universe. It is a fair distance to the next town of major interest, Andahuailillas. The 17th-century Jesuit church here is often described as the 'Sistine Chapel of the Southern Hemisphere'. The superb frescoes and paintings in the church have yet to be fully restored, but they are still well worth a visit.

Some of the best scenery of the whole trip lies beyond Huambutió. Here the superb Urubamba Valley branches off from the *Corredor Quechua* and the barren landscapes of the altiplano give way to dense vegetation; the dry air to cloying humidity; a trickle of water to the thundering course of the Urubamba River.

Another 40 kilometres (25 miles), and we're in Cusco, one of the most impressive cities in the world. I am dog-tired, and sore from 10 hours of sitting on an iron horse that could better be described as a bucking bronco, but the city of the Incas nevertheless beckons like a lighthouse to a stranded sailor.

the catchment area of Lake Titicaca. Within this valley lies the source of the River Vilcanote, which flows northwest to become the Urubamba River, eventually joining the Amazon.

The slow climb to La Raya brings us to the highest point on the line at 4281 metres (14,046 feet). A local Quechua band serenades the train, as snowcapped ranges stand out starkly in the rarefied air like cardboard cutouts on a velvet background. At this altitude you need to take things slow. The thin air requires you to breathe twice as hard to get the same amount of oxygen as at sea level. Locals drink large amounts of coca-leaf tea (which dilates the bronchial passages) to make breathing a little easier. However, it is also a diuretic so you should use it at your own risk.

ABOVE: *The astonishingly dramatic scenery of the Peruvian Andes can be enjoyed in comfort onboard PeruRail's newly appointed* Andean Explorer *on the Puno–Cusco route.*

This ancient Inca city, high in the mountains of Peru, elicits nothing but praise from all who visit. Designated by UNESCO as a 'centre of world patrimony', Cusco stuns with its sheer beauty. Baroque Spanish architecture lies layered upon Inca and pre-Inca foundations and, like a tiered cake bitten into from the top, the city reveals itself only gradually.

Prior to the Inca ascendancy in the early 1600s, the Quechuas were just a small ethnic group. Under the rule of the great emperor Pachacuti Inca Yupanqui in the 15th century, however, the Incas gained control over a third of South America, with around 12 million people under their rule. The Spanish *conquistadores*, who were greedy for gold, looked upon the capital city of the Inca as their prize goal. After the defeat of the Inca emperor Atahualpa in 1535, control of Cusco seesawed between the Spaniards and the Incas for more than 30 years. Finally the last reigning Inca, Tupac Umaru, was tried and beheaded by the Spaniards in a public ceremony in Cusco in 1572.

The Spaniards then embarked on a building spree, which included the building of the fine Cusco Cathedral that still dominates the main square. You don't have to travel far, however, to see some of the finest examples of Inca culture; the massive ruins of Sacsayhuaman, in a perfect amphitheatre on a plateau overlooking the city, are only a short drive from the town centre.

Wandering the streets of the city the next morning, I encounter an interesting assortment of travellers, artisans and musicians. It becomes evident that the Puno–Cusco railway is no ordinary train trip – my destination has becomes as important as the journey itself.

ABOVE: *A Quechua band performing at La Raya, which is the highest point (4281 metres; 14,046 feet) on the Puno– Cusco line. At this altitude the music seems to come from celestial sources.*

EUROPE

The Royal Scotsman

EDINBURGH – HIGHLANDS CIRCUIT

by Tom Savio

IN THE RAREFIED REALM OF VINTAGE passenger trains, no higher cachet exists than the appellation *Royal Train*. Great Britain marshalled the first *Royal Train* for a reigning monarch in 1843 and today stables the last brigade of royal saloons and royal locomotives for a royal family. *The Royal Scotsman* cruise train has endeavoured to be worthy of this same imperial stamp, although it caters to a distinctly republican clientele.

The similarities shared by Great Britain's *Royal Train* and *The Royal Scotsman* cruise train go beyond their names and claret liveries. Both serve as convenient stationary overnight hostelries for guests, as well as their transportation. If a royal family member is to preside over an early morning engagement in a distant shire, the *Royal Train* travels to the site on the preceding evening so the rested royal, staff and all accoutrements of state will be in place in the morning. In like manner, *The Royal Scotsman* cruise train provides its guests with an evening's refuge after the day's activities, while allowing for a morning departure to the next destination as its passengers relax over a breakfast of Mimosas and smoked trout.

ABOVE: Royal Scotsman *chefs Nick Capon and Alan Mathieson pause for a tea-time toast.*
LEFT: *Along the Kyle Line west of Inverness, the long stark vistas seem like deserts mantled in heather. The full five-day, 1421-kilometre (883-mile) journey makes for a first-class tour of the Scottish Highlands.*

However, there are some obvious differences between these two 'royal trains' that go beyond the pedigrees of their passengers. The royal family's carriages are not nearly as smart as those of *The Royal Scotsman*. They are functional and conservatively furnished with 'nice things, nicely cared for', as the service staff from English, Welsh and Scottish Railways & Railcare are fond of saying. What is paramount is keeping to the royal's schedule, and this is accomplished by engaging a pair of meticulously maintained royal locomotives named *Queen's Messenger* and *Royal Sovereign*.

In contrast, everything on board *The Royal Scotsman* cruise train is fancywork – gold, silver, bronze and pewter – from the tiny crested sewing kits to the flamboyant table service bearing the cartouche of The Great Scottish & Western Railway Company, which with its new partner Orient-Express Hotels, Trains & Cruises owns the train. *The Royal Scotsman* excels Britain's *Royal Train* by nearly every measure except for its engines. *The Scotsman* is assigned vintage diesels suitable for the light-duty tracks of the Scottish branch lines. They are long in tooth and short on temper and it comes as no surprise that our cranky engine failed to appear as scheduled in Waverly Station, Edinburgh, delaying the *Scotsman* for nearly an hour. Finally, when all was coupled-up, five days' provisions stowed, and the guests were toasting their new adventure, the guard blew his whistle and a lone piper played a farewell air as we rolled away. Onboard were 29 Americans, three Belgians and a stylish English couple who had forsaken the family concrete business for helicopters – but apparently no royals.

A postulate of rail travel is that late trains get later, and thus we found ourselves plying the fabled metals of the scenic West Highland Line in the gathering darkness. Our destination was Inverawe and a late-hour tour of a Scottish

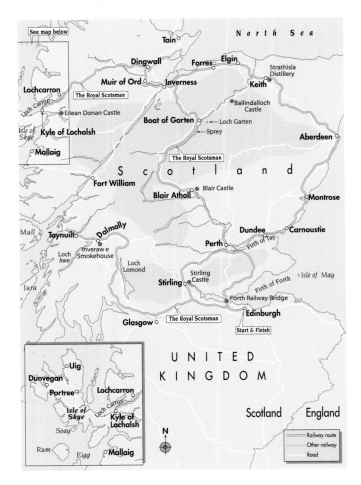

ABOVE: *From April to October of every year, the posh cabins of* The Royal Scotsman *provide travellers with an evening's refuge after the day's activities.*

smokehouse. We relied on the headlamps of our motor coach – which transferred us between railheads and attractions – to light our path. Although the splaying of salmon on a smokehouse plinth is unusual evening entertainment, our hosts, the Campbell-Prestons, must tend to their duties round the clock. In the dark, our tour took on a mystical aura and the glowing embers and clouds of steam and smoke conjured up images of Macbeth's witches.

There are essentially two schools of railway practice: North American and British. In the USA, rail joints are staggered from one side of the track to the other, producing the pleasant clickity-clack rhythm immortalized by Gershwin's *Rhapsody in Blue*. In the UK, the track joints are opposite each other, sending a jarring ka-thunk ka-thunk through the carriages. And so it was at 05:45 when *The Royal Scotsman* ka-thunked out of its overnight siding and down the branch line, jolting me from a deep slumber induced by countless G&Ts and a superb repast of roast saddle of venison.

Once back on the smooth welded rail to Inverness, we passed a steam engine puffing away in the Perth yards. Number 61264 was no apparition – it was a locomotive on holiday hauling its devotees along the quaint Scottish branchlines that had escaped the hatchet of the iniquitous Dr Beeching. In the 1960s, Beeching attempted to amputate British Rail into solvency by cavalierly lopping off branch lines. Today, despite the radical surgery, British Rail has vanished, but the late Dr Beeching remains the icon of evil, the Moriarty of railways.

Rolling up into the Highlands, the long stark vistas, shorn of trees since ancient times, reminded me of vacant deserts mantled in heather. Castles dominated their surroundings, thrusting up like craggy ghost ships on the moors. We visited Ballindalloch, ancestral home of the Macpherson-Grants. The gracious informality shown us was extended to the family dog, who had the run of the Chippendale chairs. Ballindalloch was once served by the railway, and it had an Edwardian steam locomotive named after it. A picture of the engine was among the family photos, dressed in bunting and proudly wearing a headboard proclaiming 'Royal Train'. That evening was spent on the Strathspey Railway, a museum line in the town of Boat of Garten. The industrious lads of the Strathspey earned the museum extra cash by washing the entire train by hand, and afterwards it began to rain. An old Scottish proverb says, 'If you can see the mountains, it is about to rain; if you can't, it is raining'. Nearly all the trains

and stations we passed were trimmed in the purple of Scottish thistle. Our Scottish Blue Badge Guide, Sandra Felton-Edkins, retold the thistle's legend. Once, when clandestine Viking invaders tramped through the prickly thistles, they gave out such a cry of pain that the Scottish defenders were alerted and the attack thwarted. Thus the forsaken weed became the sacred flower of Scotland.

This is a very old country, with its own indigenous animals and a compellingly sad history. Some of its unique fauna is preserved at the Highland Wildlife Park, which we visited the next morning. The shaggy Highland cattle, long-horned bovines caught in an explosion of wild red hair, were irresistible. But there were a few reminders of Scotland's unhappy saga: where crofters had lived, now sheep graze. The clans fought clans, then the clans fought the English. Afterwards the crofters were uprooted by the clan chieftains to make way for sheep in what was called 'The Clearances'. These sad tales were captured by the haunting music of Mary Strachan, who played her clarsach onboard the observation car, parked for the night on the quay at Kyle of Lochalsh. Through her harp strings, I saw a vision of sublime beauty as the misty Isle of Skye brooded over Loch Alsh.

The last full day of touring was spent viewing Eilean Donan Castle, a 'superbly romantic' 19th-century pastiche, and accidentally cooking my shoes on the hearth at Klinock Lodge during a Claire MacDonald cookery class. We began our long trip back to Edinburgh with a spectacular ride up Loch Carron and over the mountains of The Kyle Line, one of Britain's most scenic rail routes. When the line was opened in 1897, as the Dingwall & Skye Railway, it was the first significant industrial enterprise in Scotland and the most expensive railway built in the British Isles. On our final evening, when we toured the House of Chivas distillery, I noticed a portrait of Kenneth MacAlpine, Scotland's first king. I showed the picture to the British couple who had a similar surname. The lady said, 'Oh yes, that's our family' – apparently *The Royal Scotsman* had its 'royals' after all!

Dashing home the next morning we encountered two great railway engineering legends, one tragic and one triumphant. Crossing the Tay Bridge, I could see the derelict piers of its ill-fated predecessor which had disintegrated during an 1879 gale, dooming the engine, carriages and 75 passengers to the icy river below. Finally, we crossed the magnificent Forth Bridge, the crown jewel of the 19th-century railway epoch and the triumphal portal through which we returned to Edinburgh.

ABOVE: *Aglow in Dundee Station,* The Royal Scotsman *cruise train recalls the world's great evening expresses, namely* The Lark, The Night Ferry *and* The 20th Century Limited.

The Settle & Carlisle

LEEDS TO CARLISLE

by Anthony Lambert

IF A VICTORIAN CIVIL ENGINEER had been asked to build a railway through the finest scenery in England, he would probably have come up with the Settle & Carlisle line. It would have appealed to the Victorians' ambivalent feeling for wild, lonely places, fostered by the Romantic poets and painters such as Landseer or Caspar David Friedrich. However, though they admired such places, most Victorians would have taken the view that they were often better seen on canvas or from the window of a first-class restaurant car than experienced in the flesh.

Today people feel very differently, and although many travel the entire line between Leeds and Carlisle to enjoy the views, the train is heavily used by walkers to reach some of the best hiking country in England. This particular railway has become one of the best-known routes in Britain, ironically because it came near to extinction in the 1980s when British Rail tried to close it. The furore aroused by the threat made it headline news and people flocked to see this extraordinary railway through the Pennines. Thankfully the line was reprieved and the greater use of the route, for freight as well as passenger traffic, has given it a secure future.

Its inception, on the other hand, was anything but secure. The line was built by the Midland Railway, which had reached the end of its tether with the delays affecting its Scottish traffic on the West Coast main line of the London & North Western Railway (LNWR), on which it relied. Having obtained parliamentary powers to build the line, however, the Midland Railway was offered concessions by the London & North Western Railway that would have obviated the need to build the costly Settle & Carlisle. Parliament, ever desirous of greater competition, coupled with the neighbouring railways that stood to benefit from a third Anglo-Scottish main line, had other ideas. Parliamentary permission to abandon the Settle & Carlisle was refused.

The story of construction was one of heroic endeavour under appalling conditions, and the soaring viaducts and long tunnels are a major part of the railway's fascination today. It took three years more than the anticipated four to build the line, the first passenger train passing over the route on 1 May 1876. Today, a journey over the Settle & Carlisle in a howling gale or with a foot of snow on the ground might not make for ideal travelling conditions, but it gives one a better understanding of just how hard it must have been for the men building the line through such desolate landscape.

Although the line begins at the remote signal box of Settle Junction between Skipton and Lancaster, the train service from its southern end starts at Leeds. The diesel multiple units that operate most services share the line through the Aire Valley with electric trains to Skipton, pausing at Keighley, the junction for the steam-operated heritage railway to Brontë country at Haworth and Oxenhope.

A foretaste of the high standards set for the engineering and architecture on the Settle & Carlisle may be had from the

---

ABOVE: *A Settle & Carlisle train runs through typically beautiful countryside at Keighley en route to Leeds.*
RIGHT: *The now-closed station at Crosby Garrett was one of the few stations that was close to the community it served, clustered around the six-arch viaduct.*

splendid station buildings at Hellifield, with decorative spandrels supporting the canopy along the platform. Heavy ploughs were based at Hellifield to combat the snow that threatened to close the Settle & Carlisle before the advent of milder winters. At Settle Junction, the Settle & Carlisle begins its 24-kilometre (15-mile) climb at 1 in 100 to Blea Moor Tunnel, known to enginemen as the 'Long Drag'. The line soon

reaches the delightful market town of Settle, one of the few communities that contributes passenger traffic. Entering the Yorkshire Dales National Park, the line crosses a loop in the River Ribble on its meandering way to the sea near Preston.

As the landscape opens out into the rugged, treeless moorland rising above stone-walled pasture that characterizes much of the Settle & Carlisle, the jelly-mould shape of Pen-y-ghent (694 metres; 2276 feet) comes into view to the northeast. Nearby are the peaks of Whernside and Ingleborough, on which the foundations of first-century circular huts may still be seen. If people know of only one place between Leeds and Carlisle, it is likely to be Ribblehead. The viaduct to the north of the station became the centrepiece of the battle to save the line

ABOVE: *Among the fells in Upper Dentdale – an early morning Carlisle bound train crossing Arten Gill viaduct. The soaring viaducts and tunnels, built under appalling conditions, are part of the fascination of this railway today.*

because it was the cost of repairs to the 24-arch viaduct that was cited as the main reason for closure. Put at £4.25–6 million by British Rail, they eventually cost £3 million. The shantytown that once stood beside the viaduct was home to 2000 builders who toiled on the viaduct and Blea Moor Tunnel to the north.

The wind can gust at up to 145 kph (95 mph) around the viaduct, compelling railwaymen to cross on their hands and knees. Just after the viaduct, the line passes the lonely signal box and sidings of Blea Moor, where a row of derelict cottages once housed the signalmen before the days of car transport. The line then enters a cutting leading to the portal of Blea Moor Tunnel in which the climb from Settle Junction ceases and the line descends briefly to Dentdale and the Eden Valley. The 2.4-kilometre (1.5-mile) tunnel absorbed more than a third of the total cost of the Settle & Carlisle – the rock was so hard that every inch had to be blasted, and the tunnel had a notorious reputation in steam days for the way smoke lingered, despite the three ventilation shafts. The train emerges to sweep round the contours of Great Knoutberry Hill with fine views to the west over Whernside and down to the tiny village of Dent, served by the highest station in Britain, where the stationmaster's house was a pioneer of very necessary double-glazing. Snowdrifts were such a regular occurrence here that a row of stone-built cabins was erected to house the gangs of men required to keep signals and points operative during winter. Leaving Dent the train plunges into Rise Hill Tunnel. The track through the tunnel and to the north is, unusually, level, enabling the Midland Railway to site watertroughs on the approach to Garsdale, from which locomotives could replenish their tanks on the move. The line climbs again to the summit of the whole line at Ais Gill where an isolated signal box once stood, overlooked by the imposing flat-topped massif of Wild Boar Fell (708 metres; 2323 feet). It was here that the last wild boar was reputedly killed, in 1464.

The character of the line changes as the train begins its long descent to the Scottish border: copses and smooth grass cropped by Herdwick sheep, are punctuated by farms and barns amid a latticework of dry-stone walls. On the west bank of the River Eden stand the ruins of Pendragon Castle, the site where, legend has it, King Arthur's father, Uther Pendragon, was poisoned. The historic market town of Kirkby Stephen generates considerable local traffic, although the town is a sharp descent from the station. In the parish church is a representation of the Norse god Loki, unique in Britain and an example of the way Christianity sometimes absorbed earlier beliefs. Milk traffic was an important source of business for the Midland Railway, between Appleby and Carlisle; at Appleby, an entire train of milk tanks was dispatched daily until the dairy turned over to cheese production in the 1950s. Appleby has the fine remains of a 12th-century castle, which houses Roman armour, historic bicycles, a Great Hall of historic portraits and a farm for rare breeds of domestic animals. To the west are the Lakeland peaks, and the Brief Encounter restaurant in the station building at Langwathby celebrates the famous film set around the railway.

The scenery beyond Lazonby station is especially attractive, though the best way to enjoy the deep, forested gorge to the east of the line is to walk beside it on to the next station at Armathwaite, taking in the Nunnery Walks to nearby waterfalls. This marks the end of the spectacular scenery that has passed by the window since Settle, but the town of Carlisle, with its important castle, museums and art gallery should not be overlooked.

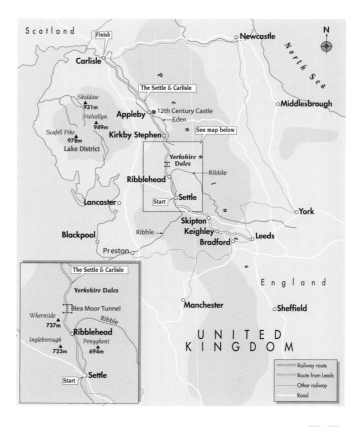

The Flåm Railway

MYRDAL TO FLÅM

by Colin Boocock

NORWAY'S STEEPEST AND MOST SPECTACULAR RAILWAY is scarcely visible from the main line train that cuts its long way from Oslo to Bergen. Passengers on the big, red *Bergen Express* will cast no more than a cursory glance at the short, dark-green train standing by the curved branch line platform at Myrdal station. Only the adventurous or those 'in the know' alight here, but they are amply rewarded for doing so.

The Flåmsbanen journey, from Myrdal to Flåm, consists of a 20-kilometre (12-mile) single-track railway that descends into a deep ravine, dropping from a height of 866 metres (2840 feet) above sea level to just 2 metres (6 feet) above sea level, where it reaches the blunt end of the Aurlandsfjord. The modern train has an electric locomotive at each end of a short chain of bogie carriages, which provide the extra power needed for the steep climb. The line has a ruling gradient of 5.5 per cent, an incline that is not far from the limit of adhesion of steel wheels on steel rails, particularly in the damp weather that is common to these parts. The railway passes through a score of tunnels that total 6 kilometres (3.7 miles) in length, and near the line's upper end the train climbs through 21 sharp bends and loops to gain height over a short linear distance.

Rail travellers changing at Myrdal for the Flåmsbanen have travelled in on the *Express* from Oslo or Bergen and will already have had a taste of the spectacular. The Bergen main line has Norway's highest railway summit at over 1000 metres (3280 feet) above sea level, where snow is not uncommon in summer. The main line was opened in 1909 and worked by steam, then diesel locomotives until electrification in 1964. In recent years the railway has been significantly improved, with efforts made to ease sharp curves and the construction of straighter diversions. Of the latter, the

new 10-kilometre (6-mile) Finse tunnel is Norway's longest and has successfully reduced travel time while protecting trains from the worst attacks of temperamental European weather.

Leaving Myrdal, the Flåm train stops a short distance away at Nåli. Here, passengers are invited to disembark and take in the thundering waterfall fed by the Flåm River. Flowing down from Lake Reinunga, the river tumbles over the rocks at this point, plunging down into a gorge. Nearby, the view along and into the valley is superb. The railway itself can be glimpsed below, hugging the side of the ravine at several levels as it weaves its way in and out of tunnels built along the sharply curved track. These loops are necessary, as the train must change direction frequently in order to gain or lose height quickly. On two occasions, the Flåm River disappears into the rock and reappears a little further on, having crossed under the railway through natural tunnels.

At Kjosfossen the water of the Flåm River is used in a hydroelectric power station that supplies the railway. As with other Norwegian railway routes, the Flåmsbanen uses

ABOVE: *The Flåmsbanen is drawn by two NSB Class 17 Bo-Bo electrics, one at each end of the train.*
LEFT: *Train No. 17.2227 at the end of the line on the harbourside station in Flåm. The Flåmsbanen completes its 20-kilometre (12-mile) journey in one hour.*

alternating current fed to the train by an overhead wire. By selecting standard railway equipment Norwegian State Railways (NSB) are able to use normal locomotives and carriages with very little modification despite the unusual characteristics of the Flåm railway.

The carriages have spacious saloons with well-spaced seats and wide windows that afford a good view. For most of the trip, the best views by far are from the west side of the train (left side on the descent, right side on a climbing train). One is always conscious of the presence of the river, whose course has eroded the rock over the ages to form this fantastic ravine. Mountains on each side rise to more than 1000

ABOVE: *Passengers cross the platform to the Flåm train. These blue carriages were borrowed from Swedish Railways for a few seasons in the mid-1990s.*
OPPOSITE: *The sides of the coaches of the Flåm railway are covered in slogans advertising the railway's exceptional features.*

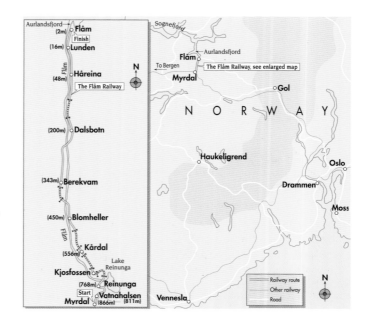

metres (3280 feet) and at certain angles of the sun, an eerie twilight settles over the valley. As the railway wends its way ever downward, nearer to the valley floor, the Aurlandsfjord comes into view in the distance.

Approaching the village of Flåm the train crosses the flat, grassy floor of the valley mouth, which remains surrounded by sheer rock faces. The final stop is the small railway station neatly arranged next to the ferry terminal at the head of the Aurlandsfjord. This fjord is an arm of water extending off the 180-kilometre (112-mile) Sognefjord, the longest in Norway. Ferries connect with some of the trains and link Flåm with otherwise-isolated villages and towns along the fjord system. The village of Flåm itself, however, is not isolated: it is on a main road from Bergen and may be accessed by way of the 11-kilometre (7-mile)-long Gudvangstunnelen which opened in 1991. Flåm station offers many modern tourist amenities including restaurants. An old electric locomotive stands on a plinth near the station and for railway enthusiasts and those with a taste for heritage vehicles there is a small railway museum. The railway depot is adjacent to the station and the spare locomotive may be serviced here while the other four remain available for the day's passenger service.

After watching the ferries depart, observing the cruise ships, enjoying a meal at one of the restaurants and looking around the railway area, what else is there to do in Flåm? In truth, not a lot. Norway's dramatic fjords and mountains are scenically magnificent, but visits to this country need to be tailored to cope with the possibility of wet or cold weather. Taking the train and enjoying the spectacular scenery from the luxury of a warm and comfortable carriage is a fine way of doing so.

FREQUENCY

The summer train service, from mid-June to mid-September, provides 10 trains each way on the Flåmsbanen, connecting with most trains on the Oslo-Bergen main line. As a result, two sets of locomotives and carriages need to be working on the branch line at the same time. The winter service is sparse with four trains each way daily and three at weekends, all covered by one train shuttling between Flåm and Myrdal. A few years ago there was a sleeping car from Flåm that was attached at Myrdal to the overnight express from Bergen to Oslo, but the service was discontinued due to minimal patronage. Despite these statistics daytime traffic on the line, particularly in summer, has necessitated lengthening the train to six carriages compared to the four used until just a few years ago.

The Flåmsbanen makes for an excellent day trip from Bergen. Alternatively, passengers travelling from Oslo to Bergen on a morning express train can fit in a return trip from Myrdal to Flåm, and comfortably reach Bergen for dinner.

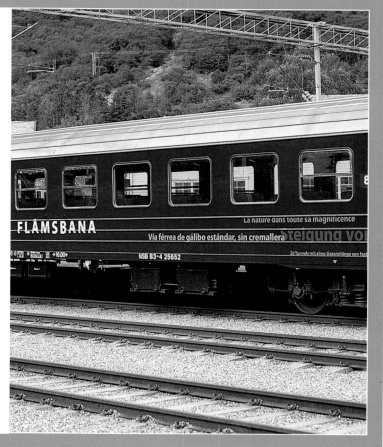

The Vivarais Line

TOURNON TO LAMASTRE

by Peter Lemmey

THIRTY-EIGHT YEARS AGO A GROUP of enthusiasts and well-wishers took over the railway from Tournon to Lamastre through the Vivarais hills of southern France. Their endeavours revived this moribund metre gauge line so successfully that it has gone on to become one of Europe's most successful tourist railways. Today it offers visitors a memorable ride with a unique blend of scenery, history and gastronomy.

France is renowned for its leading-edge railway technology, its high-speed lines and its TGV trains. In counterpoint, a day on the *Chemin de Fer du Vivarais* reflects a rather different tradition in French railways, slower paced and vernacular, but full of interest nonetheless. Away from the big cities and main lines, in what is known as *la France profonde*, the pace of life is leisurely. This is a world of hidden valleys and stone-built farms, and small towns where games of *boules* are played beneath the plane trees in the square. The journey from the Rhône Valley at Tournon to the hill town of Lamastre on the edge of the Massif Central range traverses deepest France on a train typical of French rural transport in the days of steam.

ABOVE: *A market day Billard railcar service near Tournon, the lower terminus of the Vivarais Line.*

RIGHT: *A summer morning at Tournon and a Mallet 0-6-6-0T steams away for the Vivarais hills. Travellers will be treated to a leisurely journey through vineyards and farms redolent of the Midi.*

The town of Tournon, the Vivarais Line's lower terminus, lies on the west bank of the Rhône, 80 kilometres (50 miles) south of Lyon. Its shady boulevards and red-tiled roofs give it an unmistakable feel of the Midi. There are vineyards all around and across the river on the slopes of Crozes-Hermitage the names of famous wine houses are picked out in white letters on the hillside. The station at Tournon is shared with the SNCF right bank line, now freight only; all the main line passenger traffic goes down the Rhône's left bank or the TGV route beyond.

The morning train up into the hills leaves for Lamastre at 10:00. In summer the service is extremely popular and the first train may be followed by one or even two relief services, all steam hauled. It is best to turn up at Tournon station an hour or so early, before the crowds arrive, and stroll down to the engine shed beneath the pine trees where the locomotives are raising steam. Despite its narrow gauge the Vivarais line has always needed powerful locomotives; trains on the line today load up to eight or nine coaches. The current fleet are all tank engines built to the ingenious semi-articulated design of Anatole Mallet. The senior pair was delivered to the Vivarais system as far back as 1903; two others, also Vivarais veterans, date from the 1930s. A smaller 0-4-4-0T Mallet, No. 104, is a refugee from the now-closed Corrèze system. The wooden coaches of the Tournon-Lamastre train have open balconies at each end, ideal for enjoying the scenery. From such a vantage point one can look out for the incoming Vivarais railcar, heralding its arrival at Tournon with a fanfare on its klaxon, and then watch the steam train snake out of the station with much whistling and waving.

The first 15 minutes of the run, including two short tunnels, are along mixed gauge track shared with the SNCF line. After a couple of kilometres the metre gauge swings left away

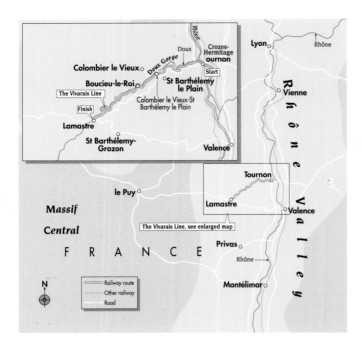

from the standard gauge and starts its climb into the hills. For a while the train pants steadily along beside the River Doux, locomotive smoke billowing away over the vineyards of the local red wine appellation, St Joseph. At Doux-Plage with its superb 16th-century bridge over the river the hills start to crowd in on either side, their terraced slopes rising steeply to the skyline. The gradient inclines further, and the sound of the engine comes back along the train as the coal smoke wafts around the coach balconies and in through open windows.

This route was once part of a much larger network known as the *Réseau du Vivarais*, 160 kilometres (99 miles) in total of metre gauge line linking a string of hill towns and villages to the outside world. Nor was the *Réseau du Vivarais* by any means the longest railway of this kind. France was once light railway country *par excellence*, covered by a vast web of metre gauge systems which filled in the gaps between the main lines and took travellers on myriad picturesque journeys off the beaten track to every corner of the country. It is this railway heritage that today's Vivarais railway keeps alive, and trains on the line are as busy now as in the light railway heyday of the 1890s when the line was built. That the Vivarais line has kept going when so many narrow gauge lines around the world have shut is something of a miracle. As early as 1955, Bryan Morgan, that inspired chronicler of branch line Europe, sensed that the closure of the *Réseau du Vivarais* was

in the offing. In his famous book *The End of the Line* he wrote an anticipatory epitaph:

...if every year the rust grows redder on the disused sidings and the moss greener on the low water-towers; if there is no scent of hot oil amid the pines and the echoes of the last klaxon-notes have died like Roland's horn between the Rhône and the Loire – then in that day, the marvellous Midi will have one marvel the less.

In fact the old system survived until 1968 and, when it did eventually close, the Tournon-Lamastre section was immediately reborn as the holiday train so many visitors enjoy today.

The section of line along the Doux Gorge must have given the surveyors a particular challenge: the railway clings to the edge of the valley *en corniche*, the river tumbling over boulders far below, while high above buzzards circle in the clear sky. At intervals the whistle from the engine can be heard echoing back off the sides of the gorge. First stop comes at a station typical of many on erstwhile light lines all over France. The plaque on the neat station house reads Colombier le Vieux-St Barthélemy le Plain, although these two villages are many metres uphill on either side of the valley. During the halt one can sit in the shade outside the Bar de la Gare and watch the engine crew rake the fire and water their charge. It is a remarkable tribute to their Swiss builders that some of the engines on the Vivarais have been working the line for almost 100 years.

Under way again after its water stop, the train winds on through the enfolding Vivarais hills; this was a region that provided a safe haven from Vichy and the occupying power during World War II. The Vivarais train was the route by which Jewish children were smuggled into the hills to be hidden by local priests, and the means by which the *maquis* secretly brought in their guns. The famous writer Albert Camus, then editor of the Resistance newspaper *Combat*, wrote later about taking the Vivarais railcar up this way when he needed to lie low.

The delightful upland scenery continues as the Mallet locomotive and its train continue the climb, through the station at Boucieu-le-Roi and on up the valley, crossing back and forth over the Doux on splendid stone bridges. Far below, swimmers and picnic parties look up and wave. After another hour or so the terminus is in sight. The train rolls slowly into the station at Lamastre, with the river on one side and the town's main square on the other. The Hotel du Midi and its rivals have for decades given Lamastre a reputation for excellent food and many of the travellers on the morning train book ahead at one of their restaurants. No doubt impelled by the thought of lunch, the train's passengers head away from the station with scarcely a backward glance and by the time the locomotive has run forward onto the turntable, peace has descended on the scene.

BELOW: *Looking smart after an overhaul, Mallet No. 414 forges up the valley past Doux Plage with a morning train for Lamastre. The train completes the 33-kilometre (20-mile) journey in two-and-a-half hours, and trains depart from April until August of every year.*

Along The Rhine

COLOGNE VIA MAINZ CIRCUIT

by Colin Boocock

MY FAVOURITE RAILWAY STATION IS COLOGNE'S (Köln's) Hauptbahnhof, situated right alongside the city's fantastic Gothic cathedral. What better place to begin an exploration of the banks of the Rhine? Ensconced in a smooth-riding air-conditioned railway carriage, I settle back into my comfortable seat having just enjoyed a tasty meal laced with a fine German Riesling. Alongside, through a large picture window, I observe some of Europe's most spectacular river scenery: the sun glints off the surface of the rolling waters; stone towers mark the heights above sharp bends in the river; castles and ancient mansions stand guard on small islands, on headlands and at the river's edge as the magnificent Rhine cuts its sinuous course beside me.

I've decided to splash out on a ticket for a ride on one of Germany's sleek, high-speed, streamlined super-trains: the *InterCity Express* on its way from Berlin to Munich. Entirely white, with only an elegant red line along the side of the carriages, the train looks like something out of the future. Inside, the carriages are spacious, with comfortable seats and plenty of legroom. The ride is surprisingly silent, the 'hush' adding to the overall impression of smoothness. Just inside each doorway is an electronic display with information about the train's timetable and an illuminated map that plots progress along the route: this train stops only at Bonn and Koblenz on the Rhine Gorge.

The Rhine is one of Europe's greatest rivers, stretching over 1320 kilometres (820 miles) from source to mouth. It begins in Switzerland as two small mountain streams and by the time it reaches Basel it has swollen to fully navigable width and depth. Swiss passenger liners, and French and German freight barges ply northwards as the river widens almost imperceptibly with each passing kilometre. At 530 kilometres (329 miles) from its source, twisting away from the German border with France, the Rhine passes the industrial town and wine centre of Bingen and enters the green-banked valley that soon narrows to form the Rhine Gorge. At this point the river becomes one of Europe's major traffic thoroughfares – not only

is there a sizeable volume of shipping, there are main roads on each river bank and main line double-track railways as well. The five main traffic arteries, constrained to run parallel to the gorge, ensure that there is plenty of movement at any time of the day or night, a thousand journeys in every hour.

I reluctantly take my leave of the *InterCity Express* at Koblenz, a large city with an interesting old town centre that warrants a few hours' stroll. Originally a Roman city, then medieval, Koblenz is dotted with a number of Gothic churches. As it has several reasonably-priced hotels, and as right bank railway services also set off from here, the city can be a base for exploration on both sides of the Rhine.

After a morning of sightseeing, I catch one of the local trains that run every hour, stopping at most stations along

ABOVE: *Speeding along the left bank of the Rhine at Oberwesel, the passengers in this InterCity train from Munich to Dortmund have a great view of the passing river. The train is passing Katzenturm (Cat's Tower).*

LEFT: *The spectacular Rhine, river of a thousand journeys, winds its languid way through the gorge. Climb aboard any number of local trains to enjoy the sights each bank has to offer.*

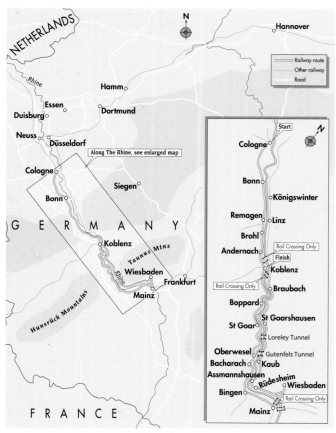

the Rhine to Bingen and Mainz. The train has only three carriages, but they are extremely modern double-decker affairs, affording an excellent view from the upper decks and ideal for watching the passing scenery. The popularity of these trains is evident as both locals and tourists use them for short hops between nearby towns and villages. A former East German Railway Class 143Bo-Bo electric locomotive alternately pulls or pushes the train – even when it is attached to the back of the train, the driver sits in his streamlined cab and controls the locomotive from the front carriage.

I decide to explore the left, or west, bank of the river. After only a few stops the train pulls in at Boppard, a town that boasts a wealth of tourist attractions, including the Kurtrierische Burg, a castle dating back to the 14th century, and the Marienberg monastery founded in 1125. There is also a chair-lift to an elevated lookout point at Gedeonseck. A few kilometres further on at Bad Salzig the river narrows, and I observe with interest as convoys of barges are split up to enable them to safely navigate the rapidly flowing water through a series of river bends. Just north of the famous Loreley rock, a mountainous outcrop that juts out, forcing the river to make a sharp detour, are the twin villages of St Goar and St Goarshausen, on opposite sides of the gorge; the right bank railway tunnels under the Loreley at this point. The sun highlights serried ranks of bright green vineyards climbing steeply up the valley slopes, their precious fruit catching the

best of the day's sunshine. Down below, the pleasure cruisers and heavy freight barges churn up water as they thrust their way through the often crowded shipping channels.

At Oberwesel, I disembark and spend the afternoon exploring. Strolling along the ancient town walls, I climb up to the top of one or two old lookout towers for a wider, panoramic view of the river threading the gorge and the twisting pattern of roads and railway tracks on either side. This is the perfect location for a bit of trainspotting – four or five InterCity trains and two local trains pass in each direction every hour. Heavy freight trains on the opposite river bank plunge into the tunnels that take the railway under the Gutenfells hillside. In the late afternoon, I catch the local train to the small town of Bacharach and find an excellent little riverside hotel. That evening, sated after a sumptuous meal, the low rumble of trains passing along the tracks lulls me into a deep sleep.

The sights of the right bank are beckoning and I take a shortcut across the river on a car ferry from Bingen to Rüdesheim. One of the highlights of this city is the Rheingauer Weinmuseum. This ancient castle is now a museum dedicated to the history of wine-growing in the Rhine, Main and Naher regions. From the roof there is a splendid view of the vineyards and a chairlift across the way that takes visitors up to the Germania monument, overlooking the river valley. The next northbound train carries me a few kilometres further down the line to Assmannshausen, where numerous riverside hotels and restaurants front the tortuously narrow streets winding their way behind the railway and up the side of the valley. Travelling further north, the local train stops less frequently as the number of riverside towns dwindles. In Braubach I visit the Marksburg Castle, which is said to be the best-preserved edifice along the Rhine. The castle's fascinating rooms include highlights such as the Knight's Hall, the chapel, the keep and displays of weapons and chastity belts! It also affords excellent views of the Rhine and the surrounding countryside.

Making use of the relatively frequent trains along the Rhine has made this a journey of discovery. Deutsche Bahn has a well-deserved reputation for good service, timekeeping and clean trains. Its nationwide network is constantly being updated and the most modern high speed trains rub shoulders with 50-year-old branch line trains, linking up with an array of useful connections. Simply passing through on an express train will give you only a fleeting impression of the Rhine Gorge, and it is well worth spending a few days to soak up the history of this region at leisure.

TOURING BY TRAIN

The Rheinland-Pfalz Ticket, sold at Deutsche Bahn stations in the area, allows an individual, a family or a group of up to five adults access to all local trains and many buses in the locality: it is valid for one weekday. For weekend travel, the Deutsche Bahn offers a *Schöneswochenende* ticket, which covers the entire country's railway network of local trains. By hopping between trains stopping at main centres it is possible to travel all over Germany at very low cost.

The Glacier Express

ZERMATT TO ST MORITZ

by Anthony Lambert

SWITZERLAND'S MOST FAMOUS TRAIN has played host to millions of passengers since it was inaugurated in 1931, the year after the last section of railway was opened to complete a metre gauge route between Zermatt and St Moritz. The journey between these two famous resorts has the distinction of being probably the world's slowest express train, but it would be a dull soul who would have it shortened. It is a measure of the fantastic scenery Switzerland has to offer that there is hardly a moment in the entire eight-hour journey when the view from the carriage window is anything but a delight to the eye.

The energetic traveller could have breakfast at Gornergrat, the summit of the rack railway from Zermatt which provides glorious views of the Matterhorn. The hotel terrace above Europe's highest open-air station at 3029 metres (10,145 feet) is the perfect place to watch the sun rise over the celebrated peak. Zermatt itself is the largest of Switzerland's car-free resorts, and a wonderful advertisement for the benefits of excluding motor traffic. Walking the narrow streets of the old village, you can still find farmyards with livestock, giving

ABOVE: *The* Glacier Express *reversing at Brigg. Daily the train makes a return trip along the spectacular 298-kilometre (185-mile) line through the Swiss Alps from Zermatt to St Moritz.*
RIGHT: *On the* Glacier Express *route a St Moritz-bound narrow gauge gingerly crosses the famous Landwasser Viaduct, which has become an icon in the promotion of scenic Swiss railway journeys.*

the place the welcome character of a rural town, rather than a resort devoted solely to tourism. The Alpine Museum tells the story of the first fateful ascent of the Matterhorn in 1865 and of the many who followed in the footsteps of Edward Whymper and his party.

As the small electric vehicles that have brought passengers' luggage to the station return to their hotels, the doors of *The Glacier Express* close with Swiss synchronicity and the train glides out of the station. For the section of line as far as Visp, the railway follows and frequently crosses the narrow valley of the Matter Vispa River, which becomes the Vispa after its confluence with the Saaser Vispa at Stalden-Saas. The course of the river as well as the route of the road and railway have changed over the years, due to the colossal avalanches that periodically engulf the valley. Their impact can still be seen in sweeping curves around the massive rock falls. Waterfalls cascade down the mountainsides, and the villages still have barns mounted on staddle stones to deter rodents.

The train's steep descent is made possible by the rack-and-pinion mechanism: a toothed bar placed centrally between the rails is engaged by a pinion on the train, helping to brake on the descents and allowing the train to claw its way uphill using the powered cogwheels. The scale of the mountains towering above the line can be properly appreciated thanks to the generous glazing of the special panorama cars which make up part of the train. Through the upper windows of these cars, some of the highest vineyards in Europe may be glimpsed as the train approaches the village of Stalden-Saas and its graceful masonry arch across the river.

At Visp, the railway joins the Rhône Valley and turns northeast to run parallel with the main line from Geneva and Lausanne into the historic town of Brig. The south ramp of the Lötschberg line as it descends to Brig from the summit tun-

nel can be seen on the opposite side of the valley. The *Glacier Express* reverses direction at Brig on the Matterhorn-Gottard-Bahn (MGB). As the line cuts a horseshoe loop around the town through Naters station, the northern portals of the Simplon Tunnel on the Bern–Milan line can be seen to the right.

The light industrial character of the Rhône Valley west of Brig is left behind as the line starts its climb to Realp through pastoral country. The river is seldom out of sight and the railway runs at a higher level than the parallel road, affording passengers spectacular views of the valley below. The first spiral tunnel is negotiated just after Grengiols station, the line looping over itself to gain height. The slopes of the valley take on the appearance of crumpled green velvet and the number of farm buildings dwindle as the railway climbs steeply to Fiesch, starting point for the cablecar journey up to the Aletsch Glacier, Europe's longest tongue of ice at 24 kilometres (15 miles).

The valley gradually broadens and the clustered villages grow larger with the greater amount of land available for agriculture. The train stops briefly at Oberwald, once

---

RIGHT: *Connecting with* The Glacier Express *at its terminus at Zermatt is the Gornergrat Bahn, a rack mountain railway that presents travellers with the most spectacular views of the Matterhorn.*

the start of the rack section up to the Furka Tunnel and the descent down to Realp, a stretch so exposed to winter snows and avalanches that it had a temporary bridge that was dismantled every October and reassembled in May. To overcome the seasonal limitations on the operation of the railway, a new base tunnel was built between Oberwald and Realp. When this 15-kilometre (9.5-mile) tunnel was opened in 1982, the line via the Furka Tunnel closed and a portion became a museum railway.

The Glacier Express reaches the junction of Andermatt where a link with the Zürich–Milan line threads the Schöllenen Gorge. The climb out of Andermatt is one of the most extraordinary sections of track as it weaves through four half-spirals to climb about 500 metres (1640 feet) in 10 kilometres (6.25 miles) to the highest point on the journey at Oberalppasshöhe (2033 metres; 6670 feet). Lunch is usually served after Andermatt, using the famous angled-stem wineglasses to counteract the gradients. The train descends the valley of the Vorderrhein to Disentis, overlooked by the white walls of a Benedictine monastery and the start of the Rhätische Bahn, which operates the line for the rest of the journey to St Moritz. Rolling farmland and woods precede one of the highlights of the journey, the gorge of Flims in which bizarrely eroded near-white walls of rock dwarf the train. Although Reichenau-Tamins is the junction station for St Moritz, *The Glacier Express* bowls across a flat industrial section to Chur, capital of the canton of Graubünden and junction with the standard gauge railway from Zürich. The train reverses and retraces its steps to Reichenau-Tamins before turning south along the valley of the Hinterrhein. Forested slopes and frequent waterfalls drop down towards the railway as it joins the Albula River near Thusis, and the line affords a constantly changing panorama of narrow valleys and mountain ranges, sometimes capped by a romantically sited castle.

The immensely dramatic Landwasser Viaduct – a sweep of slender stone arches that curve around before diving into a sheer wall of rock – bears the line over the river of the same name. Trains emerge from the tunnel to halt at the junction of Filisur, a charming village which marks the start of the climb to the Albula Tunnel, described as one of the railway wonders of the world. To reach the summit at Preda without rack assistance, the engineers contrived an ingenious series of loops and spiral tunnels, raising the line a vertical height of 416 metres (1364 feet) over just 13 kilometres

(8 miles). Even with a diagram, passengers are bewildered by the twists and turns. In winter, sledges can be hired at Preda station so that people can toboggan down the adjacent road, which is closed to traffic. Special trains are run late into the night to ferry them up the hill for moonlit runs.

From the 5.9-kilometre (3.6-mile) Albula Tunnel at the summit the train descends to the upper Engadine, one of the most delightful parts of Switzerland. At Samedan the railway from Chur joins the Scuol-Tarasp line for the last few miles to the terminus at St Moritz, one of the world's most famous winter sports resorts. St Moritz is the start of two other spectacular journeys, to Tirano in Italy by the *Bernina Express* over the highest rail crossing of the Alps; and to Scuol-Tarasp. Even after eight hours on the train, most visitors can't resist more of Switzerland's remarkable railways.

El Transcantábrico

SANTIAGO DE COMPOSTELA TO SAN SEBASTIÁN

by Eugeni Casanova

MY ARRIVAL IN SANTIAGO DE COMPOSTELA, a magnificent city tucked away in the northwestern corner of Spain, is full of surprises. Intent on boarding the train, I find myself being led not to a station, but to a 15th-century palace; instead of a porter, an elegant *maître d'hôtel* bows a welcome and leads me to a table framed by a large picture window facing onto the town's main square. Looking out onto the Plaza del Obradoiro, my eyes linger over the architectural wonder that lies across the square. In front of me is the baroque façade of the cathedral where, tradition has it, the apostle James is buried. Pilgrims from all over Europe have met here for over 1000 years, always properly attired in the traditional hat and cloak adorned with a *vieira*, a shell which is the symbol of their devotion.

My current vantage point is no less impressive – this old hostel, the Reyes Católicos, has been converted into a Parador Nacional, one in a chain of majestic old buildings across Spain that today function as state-owned hotels, combining history and excellent service. Glancing around the elaborate restaurant at my fellow passengers, the surroundings suddenly seem appropriate: it appears *El Transcantábrico* does not cater to travellers, but rather to guests; individuals who come in search of comfort and relaxation, and for whom the actual journey provides the final decorative touch to an entirely luxurious escapade.

After lunch, we take a bus to Corunna, where we get our first glimpse of the sea. Our itinerary includes a sail across the port's fjord, and thereafter a luxurious bus takes us into the station of Ferrol, where *El Transcantábrico* awaits us. More surprises – the train is much smaller than any of us had imagined; it looks like a miniature. It runs on a narrow gauge railway with only 0.914 metres (3 feet) between the rails.

Size, however, does not impact on the train's stature, its Lilliputian proportions merely adding to its charm. *El Transcantábrico* can, after all, only accommodate 48 passengers.

Our reception on board the train is celebrated with champagne, and we then take possession of what will be our little palace for one week. *El Transcantábrico* has ten carriages, four of which are saloon cars; two are set up for entertainment, including bars and a dance floor. Breakfast is served on the other two saloon cars. The train's comfortable suite compartments have a double bed, wardrobe, writing desk and telephone with an outside line. Their private bathrooms each have a hydro sauna and steam bath, and a toilet. Standard compartments each accommodate two people in bunk beds, and each standard carriage has two showers and two WCs, which are shared between the six rooms.

Bulls and guitars, an arid country burned by the sun; this is most people's image of Spain. A journey on *El Transcantábrico*, however, reveals something quite different to this cliché. Spanning nearly 1000 kilometres (620 miles) of the Cantabric

---

ABOVE: *Locals admire one of the distinctive coaches of* El Transcantábrico, *halted in a station.*

RIGHT: *A sign in one of the restaurant coaches of the train succinctly communicates the spirit that this luxury train's management wishes to offer:* 'El Transcantábrico, *a cruise by train'.*

coast, from Galicia to the Basque country, this hugely varied journey takes you through rolling green hills, beneath steep cliffs and mountains, past extensive wetlands and along sandy beaches. The route embraces four languages and as many cultures, in addition to an enticing array of gastronomic and architectural delights.

The venue selected for our first dinner is, naturally, the best restaurant in Ferrol (another Parador), and the menu is entirely comprised of seafood – the most popular Galician speciality. Travelling on *El Transcantábrico* means all meals except breakfast are eaten in restaurants, and much excellent local cuisine is sampled. After a sumptuous meal washed down with good Rioja wine, we return to the train ready for bed. *El Transcantábrico* remains standing at a different station each night, careful to let passengers rest without being disturbed by the clatter of the train on the tracks.

Our rail journey begins the next morning; while we breakfast the train stretches slowly over long iron bridges, seemingly flying high above the *Rías Altas* (high fjords) as we pass through Galicia. We stop in the small fishing port of Ribadeo, sheltered between the mountains and the sea. After a relaxed stroll through the old and winding streets of the village, we rejoin the train to cross a bridge over the estuary of the River Eo, into Asturias. The entire journey unfolds at this leisurely pace, as the train averages only 50 kilometres (31 miles) per hour. Established in 1982 and designed to enable its passengers to enjoy the scenic wonders of the northern Spanish countryside, *El Transcantábrico* was the first Spanish train to cater purely for tourists.

After a night in Luarca, we travel to Cudillero, a beautiful fishing port where the houses hang dramatically over the sea cliffs. We stop for the night in Oviedo, the capital of

Asturias. Dinner is another short bus journey away in Gijón, at the Parador Nacional on the Parque Isabel la Católica.

On the morning of the fourth day we travel to Arriondas, where the bus takes us high up into the mountains of the Picos de Europa National Park. Here, nestled among lakes, lies the highlight of the outing, the Covadonga Sanctuary. Local legend claims this as the starting point of the Christian conquest of the Moorish Iberian Peninsula over 1100 years ago. That evening in Llanes, live music emanates from the bar car as our guide organizes a series of entertainments. This is not a trip for adventurers; it is rather for persons wishing to relax, be pampered and entertained in style. As my fellow passenger, the Mexican executive of the largest beer company in Latin America told me, he has quite enough adventures during the course of his working year. He and his wife undertook this journey to get to know the country of their grandparents.

The following day brings us to Cantabria, where we pass the stunning Canyon of La Hermida. From here the track cuts its way between the mountains and the coastline, stopping at picturesque towns such as Santo Toribio de Liebana, where we visit a well-known sanctuary.

Dinner on the fifth day is considered to be one of the

highlights of the journey. This is not purely for the food, but because it takes place in the most magnificent setting one can imagine: a villa called *El Capricho* (the caprice) designed by Catalan architect Antoni Gaudí. Situated in Comillas, a coastal town well known for striking art nouveau buildings, the villa has been transformed into a restaurant. We are rendered speechless by what appears to be a fantastical dream made real in tiles and stone.

The next day we travel to Santillana del Mar, one of the best-preserved medieval villages in Spain. The nearby Altamira Caves contain the best Neolithic paintings in southern Europe, with enormous bulls and deer coloured in red and black, dating from about 20,000 years ago. After lunching at another Parador, we go on to Santander. This imposing coastal city boasts a lively casino where, after dinner, passengers may rub shoulders with the rich and famous.

On day seven we reach Laredo, where we embark on a short boat crossing to Santoña, with its extensive wetlands and beaches. Here we visit an anchovy factory, local fortresses and the church of Santa Maria de Puerto with its wonderful Flemish altarpiece. That afternoon we reach Basque country and the final leg of the journey. The Basques speak what is perhaps the oldest language in Europe, Euskara, unrelated to any other and with no known origin. They have a pre-Indo-European culture and a strong sense of independence, but what visitors will appreciate most is the region's legendary cuisine. If the whole trip has been a feast of flavours, in Basque country we are witness to an explosion of colours and light. Our rail journey ends in Bilbao, a modern and sprawling industrial metropolis. A visit to the famous Guggenheim museum, designed by Frank Gehry, is mandatory.

On day eight we are bussed to San Sebastián, the most stunning and delicate of Basque towns with its stately buildings and squares, set between La Concha Bay and mounts Urgull and Igueldo. Here we conclude our trip with a fine lunch at the elegant María Cristina Hotel.

OPPOSITE TOP: *El Capricho (the caprice) is one of the best known works of Antoni Gaudí, the foremost of Spain's* modernista *(art nouveau) architects.*
RIGHT: *A characteristic clock at one of the stations on the Transcantábrico line.*

Al Andalus

SEVILLE – ANDALUCIA CIRCUIT

by Eugeni Casanova

MODERN-DAY ANDALUCIA DERIVES ITS NAME from the old Arabic 'Al Andalus' as the Moors controlled this land for more than seven centuries until 1492, when Christians from the north ousted the last remaining Moorish king from Granada. Today, this region keeps its singular heritage and famous monuments very much alive, and the *Al Andalus* train journey visits all of its mythical cities: Seville, Córdoba, Granada, Ronda and Jerez.

In 1985, RENFE, Spain's national railway company, decided to introduce a journey that would revive the atmosphere of the glorious railway era. To this end, they rescued antique deluxe carriages, restored them, provided them with excellent service staff and ran this rolling museum along the most popular sightseeing destinations in southern Spain. With these features, the project's success was guaranteed.

Of course, taking the *Al Andalus* is not the cheapest way to explore Andalucia, nor the most adventurous. But the journey is not designed for the bold – this is unadulterated luxury – and for many that is the most exciting incentive of all. The train has twelve carriages in total. There are five *belle époque* sleeper cars (some of them were used by King George V of England to travel from Calais to the Côte d'Azur), two restaurant cars, a games saloon, a bar car, a staff car, and best of all, two shower cars – a unique addition providing an amenity foreign to the 'glory days' of train travel. The interiors of the carriages are adorned with marquetry designs, typical *belle époque* decorations and mirrors, and the 'walls' and furniture are made of rare woods. *Al Andalus* is as comfortable as a hotel on wheels.

The Art Deco carriages that make up *Al Andalus* were constructed between 1920 and 1930, and the train stands rather incongruously at the platform of Santa Justa, one of the most modern and impersonal stations in the

country. Santa Justa was built to shelter the AVE, the high-speed train that travels between Seville and Madrid, inaugurated for the World Expo that took place in Seville in 1992. The Andalucian capital, with its gothic cathedral that has a Moorish bell tower, its tapas taverns and white houses with patios full of flowers, serves as the starting point for the journey across *Carmen*'s Spain. Bulls, flamenco, gypsies and *bailaoras* (dancers) are not only the stuff of Spanish folklore – in Andalucia they are as real as the skyscrapers of New York and the windmills of Holland.

Our first destination is Córdoba, upstream along the Guadalquivir River from Seville. Lunch is served en route and the fare is 100 per cent Spanish, with *paellas*, *gazpacho* (a cold tomato soup), *jamón* (cured ham) and wonderful *asados* (roasts). After lunch, we are treated to a tour of the city. The imposing prayer hall of the Mezquita de Córdoba is certainly the masterpiece of Moorish architecture in Spain. Built in AD780, this mosque was the world's largest for many centuries, and to this day few can compare. When the Christians conquered the city in 1236 they placed their own cathedral

ABOVE: *Belle époque screen decorations are a feature of the beautifully restored interiors of the wood-panelled antique carriages of* Al Andalus.
LEFT: Al Andalus *stands on the platform at Ronda beneath a waxing moon on day four of its 855-kilometre (530-mile) six-day tour of the most famous sights of Andalucia.*

inside and the superb building was saved. The result is rather strange – at the centre of a vast hall decorated with arabesques and Moorish arches there stands a gold-bedecked Christian church. The Mezquita lies at the heart of the Old Quarter, amid quaint buildings and stark white houses dotted with colourful flowers and plants.

Under Moorish rule Córdoba was a refined city where Christians, Jews and Muslims co-existed, until the intolerant Castilian kings did away with all but Christianity in the 1200s. The Jewish Quarter, where the 11th-century philosopher and physician Avicena lived and taught, remains. We stop at a restaurant in one of its narrow alleys for a truly Andalucian meal, accompanied by a spectacle of guitars, flamenco songs and dancing.

The Andalucian countryside is covered in olive trees. Vineyards, wheat and sunflower fields also stretch for miles. Large black bulls graze peacefully next to sheep. Some day soon, they will be sacrificed for sport in the ring. Day two finds us in Granada, where we visit the famous Alhambra. With its robust walls, fine palaces, delicate gardens and magnificent fountains, this is one of the greatest examples of Moorish architecture in the world. A local saying goes: 'Give the beggar some alms, woman, for there is no pain in life like being blind in Granada'.

Perched on a hill against the backdrop of the Sierra Nevada, the Alhambra was built by a succession of rulers. The Nasrid king Ibn Al-Ahmar built the impressive walls of the Alcazaba and diverted the Darro River to provide the hilltop with water. The lovely, intricate buildings of the Casa Real were built in the 14th century, notably by Yusuf I. The Spanish rulers Ferdinand and Isabel lived in

ABOVE: *The very Moorish Patio de los Arrayanes, with its reflecting pool, in the Comares Palace of the Alhambra complex in Granada.*
OPPOSITE: *The cliffs of the Tajo, in Ronda, are spanned by the Puente Nuevo (new bridge), built in 1793 to unite the two sides of the town.*

the palace after they conquered Granada, and their grandson Charles V added an incongruous Renaissance palace. The gracious gardens of the Generalife lie to the east of the Alhambra, and on the hill opposite is Albaicín, the famous quarter once inhabited by the poor. Today, it is a showcase for popular Granada where real estate agents enjoy prosperous careers.

Antequera is our destination on day three. Here we spend several hours at a farm called La Bobadilla, where we enjoy a meal in a typical *cortijo* (farmhouse). Ronda, our destination on day four, boasts the oldest bullring in Spain, constructed in 1793. We are, of course, invited to visit its taurine museum. A balding gentleman from Madrid laughs aloud as he observes a group of North American and German tourists ooh-ing andah-ing in unison every time they come across a desiccated bull's head – they are much bigger than anyone had imagined. The most spectacular sight in Ronda, however, is the ravine that cuts the city in two. The famous Puente Nuevo, a stone bridge dating back to 1793, and which took 42 years to build, spans its steep limestone cliffs. The architect, Martín de Aldehuela, fell to his death while inspecting his finished work. That evening the train halts at Marchena. The bus takes us to Carmona where we partake in an outstanding dinner at the Parador Nacional Alcázar Rey Don Pedro. A *rociero* choir (named after Rocío, the most famous virgin in Andalucian tradition) gives a passionate performance of local songs.

Day five provides by far the best example of authentic Spain. We are bussed to Jerez, the birthplace of flamenco. In the morning we take in a superb show at the Royal Andalucian Equestrian School, where riders display expert horsemanship on magnificent thoroughbreds. We lunch in a restaurant full of local souvenirs and images. In the afternoon we visit a *bodega* (wine cellar), where we take part in a tasting. Then, with full stomachs and somewhat lighter heads, we return to *Al Andalus* to prepare for a gala dinner; our official farewell. This will be our last night on the train, and after a tour of Seville our six-day odyssey across Andalucia ends at Seville station.

POSTSCRIPT: the *Al Andalus* was withdrawn from service in 2006.

The Venice Simplon–Orient–Express

VENICE TO LONDON

by Gary Buchanan

THE CURIOUSLY VARIABLE WIND THAT SWEEPS up the Adriatic from Africa, called the sirocco by the Venetians whether it is cold and wet or hot and dry, had a definite chill. Autumn in Venice is brief: there are less than four weeks of it. The 'season' was over and the city returned to those who love it best, her own people. Near the Rialto, enormous white truffles assumed pride of place on vegetable barrows; oysters the size of a hand were in season; so too, were baby clams. At the post office behind the Danieli Hotel, around Santo Stefano, the air was heady with roasting chestnuts from vendors' charcoal griddles.

At the heart of the city lies the Piazza San Marco, crowned by a masterpiece of 11th-century Byzantine architecture, St Mark's Cathedral. Across this timeless square, the cafés Florian and Quadri serve cups of creamy chocolate and hot croissants to music lovers. Unique in the world, Venice's watery element demands that travellers heading for the city's only station employ the services of a water-taxi. My smooth passage along the Grand Canal, past the magnificent Palladian façade of San Giorgio Maggiore, beside the timeless Ca'Rezzonico and the Palace of the Doges, glimpsing the former homes of the Guardis, Lord Byron and Vivaldi, was in stark contrast to the choppy, murky Guidecca that stretched out behind me to the fashionable lido.

At the sweeping steps that lead up to the station, a frenzy of porters were ready to whisk my baggage to the red-carpeted reception desk emblazoned with the emotive appellation: *Venice Simplon-Orient-Express.* The words on the destination board high above the departure hall belied the grandeur of the journey I was about to embark upon: it simply stated *Venezia-Parigi-Londra/Train Riservato.* Known in its gilded hey-

day as the Train of Kings and the King of Trains, it also transported in regal splendour diplomats and duchesses, maharajahs and moguls, courtesans and couriers, private eyes and spies. Thundering across empires to the edge of Asia, the *Orient-Express* was the most celebrated train in history. Over the years the route of the *Orient-Express* changed with the vicissitudes of war, politics and economics. Other European express trains with 'Orient' in their names appeared and followed their own paths eastwards.

World War I brought the *Orient-Express* to a screeching stop, and some of the Wagons-Lits cars were expropriated by the Germans, never to be returned. In 1919, the train was largely superseded by a new deluxe *Simplon-Orient-Express* that used the Simplon Tunnel, then the longest railway tunnel in the world at 20 kilometres (12 miles). This new southern route was dictated by the victorious powers, their purpose being to connect the West with the emerging states

---

ABOVE: *The insignia of the* Compagnie Internationale des Wagons-Lits et des Grands Express Européens *dates from 1884. These handsome crests are fixed to the sides of each VS-O-E carriage.*
RIGHT: *The continental VS-O-E near the Arlberg Pass, passing through Austria on its two-day, 1703-kilometre (1058-mile) journey from Venice to Boulogne. An English Pullman train takes over in England.*

of Eastern Europe without having to traverse the territory of Germany or Austria, their once and possibly future enemies.

History narrates that World War II put much of Europe's train network in the hands of the Germans, who inaugurated a sort of Nazi *Orient-Express* from Berlin to Istanbul. But because only high-ranking German officials were privileged to use it, the train offered a risky ride; indeed Yugoslav guerrillas made it a particular target. Many Wagons-Lits cars were taken over by the German army to transport officers,

LEFT: *As visitors pass underneath the Rialto Bridge spanning the Grand Canal, they have a unique perspective onto the many palazzos that line the waterway.*

and some cars in occupied France were used as stationary restaurants and hostels. One even served as a brothel for Nazi officials. Others were stored in the French countryside, their racy René Lalique glass panels and colourful René Prou marquetry carefully removed and hidden from harm.

The Paris to Istanbul service resumed after the war, though it was no longer an all-luxury train, and passage was hampered by the complications of crossing the borders of Iron Curtain countries. As the 1950s gave way to the 1960s, air travel further diminished the appeal of international sleeper trains, and the last *Direct-Orient-Express* made its valedictory run with through sleeper service on 22 May 1977, aged 94, a shrunken outcast of the hurry-up age.

In 1883, the first train to bear the name *Orient-Express* was the brainchild of a Belgian, Georges Nagelmakers, who thought of bringing the American luxury Pullman sleeping car to Europe. His Paris to Constantinople (Istanbul) journey time was 81 hours and 40 minutes,and it was a luxury train from the outset. Also nicknamed 'The Land Liner', the *Orient-Express* has been romantically mentioned in fiction: Maurice Dèkobra's *The Madonna of the Sleeping Cars*; Agatha Christie's *Murder on the Orient-Express*; and Graham Greene's *Stamboul Train*, to name but a few. And like all good characters in romantic fiction, the *Orient-Express* was destined to reappear. It was to rise again in all its pristine opulence as a

regularly scheduled 'train de luxe', plying between London and Venice, thanks to the vision of James B Sherwood. At the celebrity-rich inaugural in May 1982, this enterprising American told the world's media assembled at Platform 8 in London's Victoria Station: 'The *Venice Simplon-Orient-Express* is resumed'. Unlike any other train in history, this restored icon of luxurious travel is an act of theatre that fully rewards the traveller's sense of nostalgia.

Stretching as far as my eye could see at Platform 2 in Venice's frenetic Santa Lucia station, the *Venice Simplon-Orient-Express* looked incongruous beside the futuristic ETR trains of Italian State Railways. The 17 cars of the illustrious *Compagnie Internationale des Wagons-Lits* awaited their guests. Waxed mirror-bright, they make up the longest passenger train in Europe. As I progressed along the dark blue and gold sleeping cars, smartly-attired stewards resplendent in light blue uniforms with gold braid and brass buttons to the neck greeted passengers. The restaurant cars and salon bar car were noticeable by their pale cream, blue and gold livery. Along the roof of every carriage the shining brass lettering

---

ABOVE: *The Pullman cars that run in the English leg of the VS-O-E from Folkstone to London date from 1925 and accommodate up to 26 passengers each.*

of the *Compagnie Internationale des Wagons-Lits et des Grands Express Européens* set the tone.

With a silken rustle, like a *grande dame* rising from a table, the *Venice Simplon-Orient-Express* slipped away at 10:42. Crossing the mile-long causeway that separates Venice from the mainland, I settled into my compartment – a jewel of Art Deco design, complete with Pullman-style table lamp and a silver vase containing an orchid. It was sumptuously fitted out with wood panelling, leather and brass, the cushions plump and opulent. The curved polished wood door in the corner concealed the original washbasin cabinet, which was stacked with monogrammed towels and designer soaps.

Most of the compartments are two-berth: an upper and a lower. The former folds away during the day, the latter a commodious settee that swivels by night to form the lower bed. There isn't a great deal of space when two people are trying to dress, but it's more than adequate for one. Doyenes of the train often take two adjoining compartments, affording the ultimate in European train comfort. Hot water and heating for the sleeping cars is supplied from individual coke boilers at the end of each carriage, which are kept topped up by the attendants – while more state-of-the-ark than state-of-the-art, it is in keeping with the train's strict adherence to the original. Toilets too, are located at the end of each carriage. I soon discovered how to operate the brass lever that lowered the window in my compartment and as the train glided across the Veneto, ripe and burnished by the October sun, I took gulps of scented air and watched Padua, Vicenza and the vineyards of Soave and Valpolicella disappear.

A brief stop at Verona allowed me the chance to glimpse the old tiled roofs of the city before the train left the main line to Milan and headed northwards towards the Brenner Pass and historical towns of Fortezza and Bolzano. A patchwork of vineyards and orchards, the countryside gave way to little villages with charming churches; high above anguine roads, castles perched on precarious eyries on the crags. We were approaching the shattered cathedrals of the Dolomites; it was time for lunch.

Passing through the bar car it became evident that this train, more than any other, has become synonymous with celebration. It appeared that every one of my fellow rail revellers was at some easily recognizable point in their lives; the just-retired school teacher who had saved a lifetime for the trip; the golden wedding anniversary couple presented with the trip by grateful siblings; the young couple embarking on married life.

The original *Orient-Express* was simply a means of crossing Europe in conspicuous comfort. It was also a favourite among heads of state and provided some legendary tales about royal escapades. King Boris III of Bulgaria not only loved riding the train but also used his regal prerogative to take over as driver and run at full throttle while travelling through his realm. On one such ride, the story goes, he narrowly missed being scalded by steam from a ruptured boiler tube. King Carol II of Romania was also a frequent passenger, sometimes accompanied not by his queen, but by his long-time mistress Madame Magda Lupescu.

The bar car is the focal point of the train and has been recreated from a first class restaurant car dating from 1931. The interior is immaculate, with side seating, small stools and coffee tables – the *pièce de resistance*, the baby grand piano close to the bar itself. As I sipped a Campari in these sumptuous surroundings, I couldn't confess to seeing any mysterious strangers – a Russian princess, English colonel or Hungarian count and countess – such characters remained buried in the pages of Agatha Christie's detective fiction. Opting for second sitting lunch, I was joined by a genial American couple. We all indulged in a shameful sensation of *schadenfreude* at the Brenner Pass, as we rolled past 5 kilometres (3 miles) of cars and trailers blocked at the constricted customs post; then the magnificent Alps.

In 1985, the decision was taken to alter the route which had given this headline-grabbing train its name. No longer would the Continental European portion run via Lausanne in Switzerland, crossing into Italy at Domodossola before journeying on to Milan and Venice. It was felt that this shorter trajectory denied passengers the best Alpine scenery and the route was changed to run via Zürich, the Arlberg Tunnel and Innsbruck. This proved so popular, with passengers able to enjoy a much longer stretch of stunning alpine scenery, that the route remains to this day.

In his train epic, *The Old Patagonian Express*, Paul Theroux wrote 'The journey, not the arrival, matters'. Here, on a different continent altogether, the observation seemed just as fitting. On either side of the train the stunning views burnt themselves into recollection: the Karewendal mountain summits illuminated by a sun long lost across some distant valley looked down on farmsteads with steep, high roofs silhouetted against pine-clad upland pastures. As we descended towards the Tyrolean

ABOVE: *Soon the pavement cafés that cluster around the Piazza Bra will be overflowing as culture vultures prepare to enjoy the Verona Opera Festival.*
OPPOSITE: *A wintry scene across the rooftops of Paris at dawn. The Eiffel Tower is one of the world's most famous landmarks.*

capital of Innsbruck, the mountains became hills and the landscape assumed a greener, softer aspect.

After a brief stop we continued along the ever-narrowing glacial valley of the River Inn before climbing once more towards the Arlberg Tunnel. It is 10.4 kilometres (6½ miles) long, and separates the Vorarlberg from the Tirol. At the ski resort of St Anton, winter had arrived early. I took the opportunity to stretch my legs before changing for dinner, but the icy Alpine air soon had me seeking the warmth of my wagon-lit.

As Switzerland sped past the windows of the salon Pullman I consulted the dinner menu. Christian Bodiguel, the train's chef for 14 years was proposing fresh *foie gras*, minty-white turbot and a mignon of Charolais beef. I decided there was little need to consult the *à la carte* menu and chose a fine bourgogne as accompaniment for the lavish array of French cheeses and devilishly-rich chocolate dessert that were to conclude this peerless meal on wheels. After a digestif in the Salon bar to the strains of Lloyd-Webber and Hoagy Carmichael, I retired to my compartment, which by now had been transformed by my steward to night-time configuration. The profusion of linen and blankets deadened any noise from the tracks and as the train continued its beguiling melody, sleep soon followed.

All night the Paris skies had been dumping rain. By morning, as the train approached the city from the western suburbs, the pavements and cobbles gleamed under a wet grey sky streaked with white and blue. The French capital offers visitors an enormous catalogue of delights: Paris is a city where one can spend hours reading newspapers in cafés; where lunch is a serious pleasure; where intellectuals are cool, not seedy; where glamour is commonplace; where art is sexy and sex is art.

Several passengers laden with Louis Vuitton luggage departed the train here, others joined for the onward journey to London. Beside the kitchen car fervent activity was underway as chefs inspected provisions before they were loaded on board. Some passengers took the opportunity of the 40-minute stop to buy a copy of their favourite newspaper, others watched the revictualling process from the privacy of their compartment as they enjoyed a breakfast of fresh orange juice and a variety of French breads.

Having negotiated the *Cienture* loop line around Paris, the train soon gathered speed as it headed north towards the Pas de Calais. Brunch was served in the Chinoise and Marquetry restaurant cars as well as in the Salon Pullman with its priceless Bacchanalian Maiden panels by Lalique. Outside, steepled villages, storied forests, vineyards and scattered lakes rushed past. At the Channel port of Boulogne it was time to bid farewell to the continental portion of the *Venice Simplon-Orient-Express* and its attentive crew. A coach transfer through the Channel Tunnel replaced the traditional ferry journey to Folkestone. While not in keeping with tradition, it does prevent delays due to the vicissitude of sea conditions, not to mention any hints of *mal de mer*.

Opulence was restored as I boarded the English Pullman train standing in solitary splendour at Folkestone Harbour Station. Ten chocolate and cream Pullman cars, each shining and polished like a new toy, reassured even the most dubious travellers – the two-hour journey to London's Victoria Station proved to be far from an anticlimax.

Boasting classical appellations such as *Phoenix* and *Perseus*, these stately Pullmans are a re-creation of once famous trains: *The Brighton Belle*, the *Queen of Scots* and the famous *Cunarder* boat trains. Evoking days of brass-edged trunks piled high on platforms; re-creating society photographs when stars of London's West End stage commuted to the coastal resorts; reminiscing an era when captains of industry travelled in style to branch offices in Britain's far-flung cities, these carriages too, have intriguing stories to tell.

While the verdant English countryside flashed past the brocade curtains of our Pullman carriage a traditional afternoon tea was served, complete with dainty finger sandwiches and scones with genuine Cornish clotted cream. A couple celebrating their honeymoon offered me a glass of champagne; it was a fitting finale to this journey on the world's most celebrated train.

ASIA

Trans-Mongolian &
Trans-Siberian Expresses

BEIJING-MOSCOW, MOSCOW-VLADIVOSTOK

by Jim Gill

BEIJING INTERNATIONAL RAILWAY STATION IS A colossal 1950s' building designed, it would seem, to cater for a suitably large portion of China's travelling population. In truth, it is a tired old monstrosity and now plays mostly second fiddle to a new city terminus of which the Chinese are very proud. In one regard, however, the old station still has the edge on its younger cousin, for it is here that one of the world's truly epic rail journeys begins and ends. A masochistic traveller can board a train on Platform 1 and six days and around 8000 kilometres (5000 miles) later find themselves in another great capital, Moscow.

It is a typically humid Beijing summer morning when I pick my way through the hordes of Chinese inside the great central hall of the station. A security check entails pushing my backpack through an antique x-ray machine, which does not appear to be plugged in or connected to any display monitor. The officer in charge is satisfied, however, and encourages me to thrust my arm into the opposite end and pull my luggage out. Platform 1 is easy to find but there are no signs to indicate the scale of the journey ahead. Anyone hoping to see 'Trans-Mongolian Express – Beijing to Moscow' up in lights will be sadly disappointed. Like the Russians, the Chinese refer to their trains by numbers, and so the great green Skoda locomotive about to haul us a vast distance is simply known as *Train No. 3*.

At 07:40 precisely, as it does every Wednesday morning throughout the year, the express pulls out of the dark terminus and begins its famous journey northwest to Mongolia. My compartment is a comfortable four-berth affair, which I share with three other westerners. There is no shower, but a boiler or samovar at the end of the carriage provides continu-

ous hot water for washing and drinks. Introductions are barely over when the train emerges from the depressing Beijing suburbs and we find ourselves in the fertile Chinese countryside, the open fields punctuated with copses of poplar trees. Excited cries herald our first views of the Great Wall, which meanders magnificently through the steep scarps. The world's greatest man-made structure has been beautifully restored close to the capital. As we travel further out though, it is often rarely more than a low pile of rubble.

I head for the dining car, which is already the hub of the train, and for some small change treat myself to a splendid banquet of meats, Chinese vegetables and fried rice. Excellent local beer and an intriguing, slightly fortified, red wine are also available. The spectacular vistas continue until sunset, by which time we are approaching the Chinese-Mongolian

ABOVE: *Apartment blocks on the banks of the Angara River in Irkutsk. Travellers on the* Trans-Mongolian Express *can transfer to the* Trans-Siberian Express, *known locally simply as* Train No. 9, *in Irkutsk.*
OPPOSITE: *In earlier days the Trans-Siberian Railway passenger trains were hauled by a succession of massive class P36 4-8-4 steam locomotives such as this one. Electric and diesel locomotives have replaced them, but the time saved on what was a seven-day trip is just one day!*

border. It is here, at the town of Erlian, that an extraordinary operation takes place. Because Chinese and Mongolian railways operate on different gauges, the train's wheel bogeys have to be changed. We shunt into a brightly illuminated shed and, carriage-by-carriage, the train is hoisted into the air by gigantic hydraulic jacks before teams of mostly female workers move in to change the wheels. Passengers are encouraged to stay onboard during the bogey-changing. You can get off, but it is a novel experience to stay onboard and feel yourself being hoisted aloft. A mere three hours later the switch is completed and we are set to continue our journey into Mongolia.

Dawn breaks and the blinds are raised to reveal a staggering transformation in the scenery. We are now in the heart of the Gobi Desert, although there is no sand. These are the Gobi's grasslands and herds of sheep and cows dot the landscape. Majestic horsemen, standing high in the saddle, muster the animals and occasionally break away to ride alongside the train. Huge steppe eagles hover above, on the hunt for marmots. There is also the odd cluster of *gers* (yurts), the traditional circular white tents that are home to the Mongolian nomads. After the congestion and confusion of China there is something wonderfully refreshing about this empty part of the world. The express now starts its climb into the Khentii mountain range and begins its approach to Ulan Bator.

ABOVE: *A beautifully restored section of the Great Wall of China, the country's most popular tourist attraction. The wall was constructed 2000 years ago, and originally stretched for a least 4000 kilometres (2500 miles).*

Mongolia's capital is an uninspiring collection of Soviet-style tower blocks and industrial buildings, although the area surrounding it is well worth exploring. In July the magnificent Naadam Festival attracts hundreds of the country's top horsemen, wrestlers and archers for three days of intense competition.

The train stops in Ulan Bator for just 40 minutes, unloading passengers and taking on fresh provisions. I have arranged to meet a friend of a friend, a Mongolian businessman called Mr Khan, who quickly seeks me out and ushers me into the back of a minivan in the station car park. In a flash he has uncapped a bottle of vodka and is pouring the contents into a silver bowl. With a big grin he thrusts it into my hands and I take a sip of the fire-water, before trying to hand it back. But the smile has been replaced with a frown and it is suddenly obvious I'm expected to down the entire contents. I somehow manage it and the grin returns, even bigger than before. Now we're off and running. My new friend downs his bowl in one and offers me

another. In 15 minutes we manage to finish the entire bottle. A glorious warm glow envelops me but my head is beginning to fog at an alarming pace and, before I know it, I am being embraced and then bundled back onto the train by the ebullient Mr Khan. My first major encounter with Mongolian hospitality is over. It may have been a little short on conversation but there was no doubting the warmth – and it enabled me to sleep soundly for the next four hours!

From Ulan Bator the *Trans-Mongolian Express* continues its northeastern route and late on the second night arrives at the Russian border. At the first stop, Sukhbaatar, Mongolian customs officials board the train and usher us out of our compartments. They check under seats and in luggage spaces, apparently searching for smuggled Chinese and Mongolian goods. Satisfied, they give us a nod and a half smile and move to the next carriage.

It is a similar procedure when the train moves across the border to the Russian town of Naushki. This time it's the Russian officials, who turn out to be more officious and very thorough in their searches. We hear a tremendous din from the next carriage and a few minutes later watch as the Russians roughly frog-march two Chinese men from the train. A stash of furs has been found, hidden behind a panel in one of the compartments, which the men had been attempting to smuggle into Russia. Three hours later, when we finally pull out of Naushki, we are minus two passengers – their fate unknown.

As dawn breaks on the third day we pass through the city of Ulan Ude, capital of the Buryat Republic. It is a pleasant

enough place though not a great deal happens here. This was emphasized during the 1990 royal visit by Princess Anne when city officials were heard to remark that it was the most exciting event since Ghengis Khan and his army marched through Ulan Ude 750 years earlier. However, just east of the city a significant moment arrives, as the Mongolian/Chinese branch line connects with the main Trans-Siberian railway.

Soon after, we get our first glimpse of mighty Baikal, the world's oldest and deepest lake. The statistics of this incredible body of water almost defy belief. Here are a few: formed almost 50 million years ago the lake is estimated to contain more than 20,000 cubic kilometres of water (12,400 cubic miles), or roughly a fifth of the world's drinking water supply. It is the size of America's five great lakes combined, and if it was emptied and all the rivers of the world were diverted to flow into it, they would take more than a year to fill it. Of the thousands of species of fish and other creatures that make it their home, more than 1000 are endemic. And despite the best efforts of Russian industry, Baikal's waters are remarkably clear and pure, thanks to the filtering action of the sponges which inhabit its depths. The lake, not surprisingly, has its own legendary monster and another myth tells how dipping one's hand in the icy waters can add a year to your life. For the next hour the train hugs the shoreline and, under an azure sky, it is easy to see why this fantastic expanse of water is known affectionately as the 'Blue Eye of Siberia'.

We pull into the mining town of Slyudyanka, and from one of the numerous traders on the platform I buy a smoked fish for next to nothing. It turns out to be omul, a relative of the salmon but another of Baikal's unique species, and a tasty staple of the local population. The Angara River, the only waterway to flow out of the lake, signals our imminent arrival in Irkutsk, the capital of eastern Siberia. The masochists stay on board as the train rattles on to Moscow. But of all the places en-route, Irkutsk is the one above all others that demands a stopover.

TOP: *Until recently the standard of food on the* Trans-Mongolian Express *was relatively poor, making it essential to bring extra provisions.* LEFT: *A carriage attendant in her claustrophobic cabin on the Trans-Mongolian Express. There are two attendants to each carriage, with one bed between them. Some make it a family affair, bringing their children along.*

The Cossacks founded the town more than 350 years ago and it was once known as the Paris of Siberia. That may be overdoing it a little but there is still a great deal of charm about the place. It is a city of delightful churches, wide boulevards and exquisite log houses, some of which date back to the original settlement.

Irkutsk is a mere 60 kilometres (40 miles) from Lake Baikal, so a day trip is mandatory. The bus deposits me in the quaint village of Listvyanka. The countryside here is breathtaking with forests of silver birch descending from high slopes to the water's edge. There is also an excellent museum which contains all you want to know and more about the immense lake, in addition to a room which holds a rather depressing tank containing two chubby freshwater seals, found only in Baikal's waters.

Sightseeing completed, and after a night's rest in the rundown Intourist hotel, I return to the station to catch *Train No. 9*. Foreign travellers call it the *Trans-Siberian Express*, while the Russians refer to it as the *Baikal*. Either way, it is generally considered to be the country's finest train and every day, from May to September (after that, every second day – subject to change), this blue leviathan rolls out of Irkutsk on its four-day journey to Moscow.

It appears at first that I have a compartment to myself, but my privacy is short-lived. I'm actually sharing with three off-duty soldiers who are on their way back to their barracks in Moscow. The boys set up camp in the dining car where they stay for virtually the entire journey, on a spectacular vodka binge. Their staying power is phenomenal. Morning, noon and night they are there, glasses full, bottle at hand, deep in conversation. I join them for an hour one afternoon but they are way out of my league. I do learn one thing though, that the world's best vodka comes from Irkutsk, is called Baikalski, and not surprisingly is distilled from the waters of the lake.

Peering out of the window, it is difficult to understand why Siberia is always associated with desolate icy wastelands. Of course, travel to the north of this vast expanse, and that is what you will find, but between Irkutsk and Novosibirsk the landscape is magnificent. Here, thick forests of aspen, silver birch and pine cover the sides of majestic river valleys that cut through the undulating terrain, the trees' red and gold

ABOVE LEFT: *Maintenance workers on the* Trans-Siberian *take a break from their duties underneath a carriage at Danilov Station.*

ABOVE RIGHT: Babushkas *touting for business on a platform in Siberia. The old ladies' livelihood depends on custom from train passengers. They sell anything from pickles to potato cakes.*

leaves providing a wonderful display of colour. Occasionally we glimpse clusters of charming traditional wooden cottages (almost all of A-frame design to afford protection from snow in the bitter winter).

We pull into the capital of Western Siberia, Novosibirsk. The station is massive, like the city itself, in fact, Siberia's largest. Now boasting a population of more than 1.5 million, Novosibirsk did not exist before the railway was built. Today, it is the industrial centre of the region. The *Trans-Siberian Express* then thunders on, affording those onboard an incredible history tour as it passes through famous cities such as Ekaterinburg, formerly Sverdlovsk, where Russia's last Tsar, Nicholas II, and his family were murdered by the Bolsheviks in July 1918. Ironically, in 1891 Tsar Nicholas had laid the ceremonial foundation stone that marked the start of construction of the great railway. Twenty-five years later this astonishing feat of engineering was completed, just in time for the revolution.

Soon after Ekaterinburg everyone jostles for position in the corridor to glimpse the famous obelisk that marks the boundary of Asia and Europe. It is not much to shout about but we celebrate anyway, this time with Russian *champagnski* – let's just say it improves after a couple of glasses. At every stop the entrances to the carriages are mobbed by *babushkas*, the old ladies who eke out a living selling homemade pickles, potato cakes and smoked fish to hungry train passengers. To be honest these delicacies are a welcome change from the staple meat and potato dishes served up in the dining car.

LEFT: *The* Trans-Siberian Express *pulls into the imposing station of Novosibirsk, the capital of western Siberia. The rest of this industrial city, which grew up around the railway, is somewhat less impressive but does boast the Russian Federation's largest opera house.*
OPPOSITE: *The carriage nameplate says it all: 'Rossiya: Moscow–Vladivostok'.*

THE TRANS-SIBERIAN PROPER

Purists will tell you, and with some justification, that to travel the Trans-Siberian Railway properly, one must complete the full journey from Moscow to Vladivostok or vice-versa. The 4000-kilometre (2486-mile) leg from Irkutsk to Russia's eastern seaboard is a three-day journey through thick taiga forests, across wide plains and along picturesque river valleys. For my journey I connected with *Train No. 2* from Moscow, *The Rossiya*.

I shared a compartment with Iain, a Glaswegian who at every stop insisted on disembarking in full highland dress and treating the locals to an impromptu performance on his bagpipes. The train has a weird effect on some people! We passed through some fascinating cities including Chita, founded by the Cossacks in the 17th century, and once an important location on the Chinese trade route. We also had the dubious pleasure of spending the better part of a day in the former military outpost of Khabarovsk, one of the brighter far-eastern cities, which believe me isn't saying a great deal. From Khabarovsk the train headed due south, hugging the Chinese border to its final destination, Vladivostok.

For decades, foreigners were barred from this famous port as it was home to Russia's Pacific fleet.

The train terminated instead at Nahodka, a dull port 220 kilometres (140 miles) northeast of Vladivostok. Nowadays Vladivostok is a far more impressive terminus, its hub being the Zolotoi Rog Bay, which means the Golden Horn. The railway station is also conveniently situated next to the ferry terminal, where the majority of foreign travellers connect with a boat to Japan.

As the train cuts through the Ural Mountains, pretty lakeside dachas, the summerhouses of the well-to-do, replace the impoverished cottages of the Siberian countryside. We are nearing Moscow and word comes from the dining car that a case of Moldovan wine has made its way on board. It demands to be tried but equally quickly screams to be dispensed with. This is clearly from the lower end of the market and fermented from something other than grapes.

We cross the mighty Volga, or 'Mother Volga' as the Russians reverently call her. Europe's longest river is 1 kilometre (0.6 of a mile) wide at this point, and yet in winter it is completely frozen over. Some 70 kilometres (45 miles) from Moscow, the magnificent domes of Sergiev Posad, Russia's religious capital, come into view. This is the signal for a burst of activity on the train as the debris of our epic journey is hastily bundled into suitcases, handbags and backpacks. Only the soldiers remain unmoved, happy to continue their own epic binge in the dining car.

We snake through the Moscow suburbs, at each stop expecting a sign of adulation, or at least acknowledgement, from the smartly dressed commuters. Don't they realize that this is the world-famous *Trans-Siberian Express*, for goodness sake? We've come all the way from Beijing. Surely they must be impressed? Apparently not – there is not a hint of recognition. To them it's just another train. To me, though, it's the beautiful big blue express, my home for the past four days that is sadly now pulling into Moscow's Yaroslavski station. Incredibly the station clock shows us to be a minute early – 8000 kilometres (5000 miles) from Beijing and a minute early! Someone really should have a word with the driver.

95

THE TRANS-MONGOLIAN & TRANS-SIBERIAN EXPRESS

Khyber Pass Line

LAHORE TO KHYBER PASS

by Peter Lemmey

THE KHYBER PASS, HIGH ON PAKISTAN'S Northwest Frontier, is the terminus of one of the world's most remarkable railways. Opened in 1926, the line up onto the Pass was a legendary feat of railway engineering through inhospitable terrain inhabited then, as now, by fiercely independent Pathan tribesmen. Today the train still provides an opportunity for travellers to make the journey and look down on the other side of the Pass into neighbouring Afghanistan.

Pakistan is a land of dramatic scenic contrasts, vivid history and strong cultural identity, and the journey from Lahore to Khyber Pass makes for an unforgettable trip. The journey falls into two parts: a diesel-hauled day's run from Lahore up to Peshawar at the foot of the mountains; and a second day for the climb from Peshawar up to the Pass itself with the bonus of steam haulage. The journey needs to be planned well in advance: the Peshawar–Khyber Pass train runs every Sunday (subject to change) and advance bookings need to be made. The entire route from Lahore is 1.65-metre (5-foot 6-inch) broad gauge, the main line standard for this part of the world, and most of it is single track.

For centuries Lahore has been the cultural and commercial capital of the Punjab and one doesn't have to look far to discover a fine legacy of historic buildings. This architectural heritage extends to the railway. In tree-shaded Empress Road are the headquarters of Pakistan Railways; the colonnaded building was once the HQ of the old North Western Railway, and visitors are still received with grave old-fashioned courtesy among the potted palms and frayed red carpets. Here one can arrange to visit two other fascinating railway establishments in Lahore, the Moghulpura railway works (where a number of old steam engines are preserved) and the railway training college at Walton. The signalling school at Walton with its vintage model railway is a particular gem. Highly

impressive too is Lahore Junction station, starting point of this trip. Few connoisseurs of railway stations will be disappointed by this extraordinary fortified building, seen at its best in the low light of dusk when its brick towers and turrets stand out against the evening sky.

The *Awam Express* (Train 13 Up) across the Punjab to Peshawar is scheduled to leave just before 06:00. It offers the traveller both Air Conditioned Class accommodation – red plush seats, a carpet on the floor and your own WC – and Economy Class which also provides an upholstered seat, but in among the throng. Travelling in Economy, be it only for some of the journey, will doubtless involve being drawn into conversation with companionable local passengers. Pakistanis relish the opportunity of a train journey to talk to strangers, particularly from abroad. English is widely spoken, and remains the official language on the railways.

If the train arrives on time from the south, it pulls away from Lahore Junction station just before dawn. The

ABOVE: *Booking clerks upholding the bureaucratic traditions of the Raj, Rawalpindi Division.*

LEFT: *Steam raises the echoes across the Hindu Kush as a pair of HGS Class 2-8-0s power the Khyber train away from Jamrud, over the first viaduct towards the Pass.*

engine is a General Motors or Hitachi diesel, built in the 1970s. American railroad buffs will want to look out, too, for the classic Alco cab units from the 1950s still to be seen on some trains. The *Awam Express* rumbles slowly out through the raffish Lahore suburbs with many blasts on the diesel's horn.

Before long the great Punjab plain is all around. On each side of the line neat fields of wheat, oilseed and sugar cane stretch away, bright green and yellow in the morning sunshine. Avenues of trees line the country roads and at level crossings passengers get a glimpse of waiting horse-drawn tongas and exuberantly decorated Bedford lorries. The *Awam Express* makes several stops en route, and although meals are available from the train's kitchen car, turbaned bearers from the refreshment rooms at the main stations of Wazirabad, Lala Musa and Jhelum will appear at the train window to offer tea and omelettes. Beyond the Jhelum River the landscape becomes less flat and the line climbs gently between sandy hills. During a 10-minute stop at the old garrison town of Rawalpindi the kitchen car is shunted off. A few miles further on the train pauses at Taxila, junction for Havelian and the Karakoram Highway, where tourists sometimes disembark to visit the famous archaeological sites. Like many of the wayside stations on the line, time seems to have forgotten Taxila. The stationmaster's furniture is marked Punjab Northern State Railway, the company that built the line in 1880s: can it all have been here since the line opened?

Late afternoon heralds arrival at one of the major landmarks on this journey. Shortly after Attock the express emerges from a rock cutting to cross a long, high viaduct. The river far beneath is the Indus, on its way from the Himalaya down to the plains, and the shadow of the train bounces along the blue-grey waters below. For generations of travellers the Indus crossing at Attock has been a symbolic spot: the transition from the quiescent well-ordered plains of Punjab to the turbulent, lawless mountains of the Northwest Frontier.

The *Awam Express* arrives at Peshawar Cantonment station at dusk. Peshawar has for centuries been a crossroads for Asian trade routes, and an intriguing day can be spent strolling through the city's bazaars and markets where everything from carpets to contraband is on offer. However, an early start is required on the morning of the Khyber train run to begin the second part of the journey.

Dawn touches the surrounding hills as plumes of steam rise from the locomotives shunting the train. A stud of HGS Class 2-8-0s is shedded at Peshawar to work the Khyber Pass service. The HGS Class was the workhorse of the Indian Empire and the train is powered by two, one at each end. At 07:00 the headlights are turned on, the guard waves the green flag and, wreathed in vapour, the train steams out of early-morning Peshawar with the engines whistling shrilly to clear the track. There is a short halt before the curious level crossing with Peshawar airport's runway while clearance is obtained from the control tower, then a second longer stop at Jamrud station. Here the train enters the autonomous tribal area; beyond this point the safety of unaccompanied travellers cannot be guaranteed, hence the platoon of Khyber Rifles that escorts the train. There may also be local tribesmen on the train, exercising their historic right to a free ride.

The two engines storm away from Jamrud towards a defile in the mountain wall ahead and the climb begins in earnest. The Khyber Pass route through the Hindu Kush mountains has preoccupied strategists since time immemorial and many invaders have skirmished through it. It was the third Afghan War in 1919 that prompted Sir Gordon Hearn's classic feat of railway engineering in building the line up through the mountains so that broad gauge troop trains could be rushed

to the frontier. The train thunders on through rock cuttings, across embankments, over viaducts and into tunnels, the sounds of the engines echoing back and forth among the hills. Twice during the morning the train has to reverse to gain height on the mountainside, the trailing engine taking its turn to lead. Signs of the region's violent history are seldom far away and the train winds past fortresses at Shahgai and Ali Masjid as it climbs towards the Pass.

Once through the Ali Masjid gorge the gradient eases and, near the end of the line, mud-walled compounds of local clans line the track; young boys hitch a ride for the last kilometre or two. Shortly before midday the train stops in the terminus station of Landi Kotal on top of the Pass. All around are the jagged peaks of the Hindu Kush and, from a nearby viewpoint, you can look down on the western side of these wild mountains towards Kabul; the grande finale to a unique journey.

ABOVE: *The train's midday halt at Landi Kotal station on the top of the Pass.*

The Darjeeling-Himalayan

NEW JALPAIGURI TO DARJEELING

by Laurie Marshall

WHERE IN THE WORLD CAN TRAVELLERS embark on a steam-hauled train journey on a narrow-gauge railway protected as a World Heritage Site, climb to just over 2256 metres (7400 feet) and pay less than three pounds sterling for a first class fare? The answer is West Bengal, India, and the railway is the Darjeeling–Himalayan, now part of Indian Railways.

The journey between New Jalpaiguri and Darjeeling takes eight-and-a-half hours. Between these two points, the diminutive two-foot gauge train runs through some of the most breathtaking scenery on this earth. The route is tortuous in the extreme; with tight curves and a climb of almost 2130 metres (7000 feet) over the first 84 kilometres (52 miles), the line loops and zigzags to gain height and crosses over the main road 120 times – small wonder highway engineers would like to see the closure of this precious railway.

To the British living and working in northern India in the 19th century, the late spring, summer and early autumn months were intolerably hot (they still are) and the string of hill stations nestling in the Himalayan foothills were retreats to comparative coolness. None more so than Darjeeling, 2130 metres (7000 feet) above sea level. Development of Darjeeling was started in 1814 by the British-owned East India Company, and in 1835 the town was selected as a sanatorium for British troops. However, the cart road from the plains was totally inadequate and the journey had to be made by carriage, taking days rather than hours. The tea industry continued to expand rapidly and, in 1879, authorization was given for the construction of a railway from Siliguri to Darjeeling. The actual building of much of the railway proved extremely difficult and dangerous; wildlife including snakes, tigers and elephants abounded, as did diseases unknown to Europeans. Additionally flooding from the monsoon rains was frequent, leading to massive landslides.

By mid-1881, the railway was fully operational but the original locomotives supplied from Britain were decidedly inadequate for the fast growing traffic. In 1889, the first of the famous 'B' Class 0-4-0 saddle tanks were delivered from Sharp Stewart & Company in Manchester to be followed by 30 more over the ensuing 54 years. It is the surviving members of these small (they weigh a mere 14 tons) but powerful engines that still carry out the bulk of the work on the Darjeeling railway today. Sadly, four diesel locomotives are now also used – however, Indian Railways has made the decision to keep some steam trains running indefinitely.

We travelled overnight on the Darjeeling Mail from Calcutta, reaching New Jalpaiguri at 08:15. The so-called 'booked connection' with the narrow gauge train is tentative and so we quickly make our way across the station, where a diminutive blue train awaits us. The train to Darjeeling comprises one first class coach, one second class coach and a baggage car. Four-coach trains are now more than the locomotives' ageing boilers can handle.

Ready to head for the foothills, the locomotive is stacked high with coal, the tiny footplate only just accommodating

ABOVE: *To ride on a first class roof you need a first class ticket!*
RIGHT: *Not all railway journeys are picturesque. Train No. 803 drifts into Siliguri Town station on its daily 88-kilometre (55-mile), eight-hour fifteen-minute journey from Darjeeling to New Jalpaiguri.*

The train used to run up to Darjeeling twice daily, but road competition has cut passenger traffic dramatically and freight conveyance by rail is obsolete. Running only once a day now, the train is still crowded but apart from tourists heading for Darjeeling, the rest of the passengers are local folk making short journeys, with or without tickets. Many of the people in these parts are of mixed origin, Nepalese, Sikkimese or Tibetan: dressed differently from the Bengalis they are less verbose but equally friendly. First-class carriages are less crowded though not sumptuously comfortable and be warned – first class tickets must be produced, even when travelling on the roof of the first class coach. Before leaving New Jalpaiguri, a visit to the office of West Bengal Tourism is advisable – a permit, generally stamped in a passport, may be necessary. The first 3 kilometres (5 miles) to Siliguri Junction are uninspiring; West Bengal is grossly overpopulated and the landscape yields little more than shanty dwellings, rubbish heaps, scruffy under-nourished children, beggars and unwanted dogs. As we head on to Sukna, 'the dry place', the track runs parallel to the main road and crosses the Panchanai River, short on water but full of playing children, before heading into tea country. It was at Sukna that the twelve-coach trains, with their three interspersed engines, used to divide. Water is taken here before tackling the next 64 kilometres (40 miles) of almost continuous climbing to the summit of the line at Ghum, 2258 metres (7407 feet) above sea level.

Tea plantations give way to dense forests of sal and toon trees, and shortly after Rangtong station we stop to take on water from the Rangtong River. The train has only covered 10 kilometres (6 miles) since Sukna but climbed over 260 metres (850 feet). After the Rangtong water stop comes the first of the six virtually unique zigzags, or 'reversals': to deal with

the driver, his fireman and a shovel. The coal is passed down through the cab windows by a man perched precariously on top of the pile, wielding a hammer to break up the larger lumps. Wet weather is commonplace above Kurseong for much of the year and at the front of the engine are two more crew who spread sand under the driving wheels if slipping occurs.

ABOVE: *Traders in Kurseong Bazaar dread the daily passing of the New Jalpaiguri to Darjeeling train, as soot often spoils their fresh produce.*
OPPOSITE: *Tea has been grown and picked in the Darjeeling district for almost 200 years; almost all the plucking is done by women.*

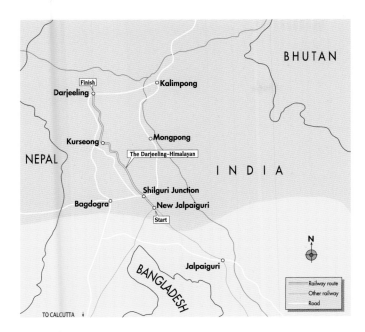

Mahanadi Valley and in the distance, the great plains of West Bengal. We sip tea and wait while the locomotive is changed for the next leg of the journey; it is late morning and we have covered 35 kilometres (22 miles).

The next 21 kilometres (13 miles) to Kurseong are the most scenic, affording stunning views of range after range of foothills, three 'reversals' and a tight loop at 'Agony Point' before water is taken from a mountain stream at Paglajora. At Mahanadi the train runs along the main street and repeats this procedure in the much more congested town of Kurseong. While the engine is serviced in Kurseong, we chat to fellow passengers over another cup of tea in the ageing station refreshment room before strolling through the bustling bazaar area. We are now 1483 metres (4864 feet) above sea level and 56 kilometres (35 miles) from New Jalpaiguri.

The journey up to Ghum produces new vistas, fir trees, tea estates and Buddhist temples, but no respite for the locomotive. At Ghum there is an extended water stop and we disembark to snap a picture of the engine standing by the faded board, which proclaims a height of 2258 metres (7407 feet) above sea level – the highest point in the world reached by regular steam train traffic. At Bhatasia, the track effects an amazing double loop and in the background a superb view of the Himalayas comes into view. Arrival in Darjeeling is uneventful – the journey is the highlight, not the destination.

the incredibly steep gradients, a team of creative engineers ran the track into a series of dead end stretches; the train runs forward into one of these sections of track, reverses up the next, then proceeds forward again towards Darjeeling. This three-way operation is conducted at considerable speed, with each shunting movement being directed by a flagman residing temporarily in a battered corrugated iron hut.

The steepest gradients on the line are between Rangtong and Chunbati. Leaving the forested area behind, the tiny train climbs towards Tindharia through two more 'reversals' and a loop at Chunbati. Superb views of the Mahanadi River Valley appear on each side as we climb. Just before Tindharia station, the train circumnavigates the hill spur upon which the extensive railway workshops and administrative headquarters are situated; admission here is granted only by prior arrangement with Indian Railways. Looking southwards from Tindharia station there are further spectacular views of the

The Royal Orient Express

DELHI – RAJASTHAN & GUJARAT TOUR

by Walter & Cherie Glaser

WHEN BRITAIN GAVE INDIA ITS INDEPENDENCE in 1948, the Maharajahs, now unable to raise taxes, were forced to give up their trains. The carriages were purchased by the State of Rajasthan for the *Palace on Wheels*. When wider-gauge tracks were laid and more modern carriages introduced, the original narrow-gauge carriages were sold to the state of Gujarat and renamed *The Royal Orient Express*. Today this is one of the very special handful of nostalgia trains still to be found around the world. Travelling across the crowded cities and open countryside of Western India, the *Royal Orient Express* journey is reminiscent of the days when this part of the world was under the rule of the British Raj and train travel for the Indian aristocracy was all about luxury, leisure and comfort.

Our rail journey across Rajasthan and Gujarat started at Delhi's Cantonment railway station. A handsome, red-turbaned, white-gloved Indian in a smart beige uniform greeted us. 'Welcome to *The Royal Orient Express*', he said with a smile, as he invited us to take a seat in the waiting room. A few minutes later our excitement mounted as, with a fanfare of hissing steam, *The Royal Orient Express* chugged into the station, drawn by a magnificent steam engine that gave it a 1930s' aura. From this moment on we instinctively knew that the 3200-kilometre (1988-mile) journey we were about to embark on would be a storybook Indian adventure.

Two turbaned porters quickly settled us into our comfortable compartment. More like personal butlers, nothing was too much trouble for them. The two single beds looked comfortable and the cabin large by comparison with other similar trains. A classic brass ceiling fan, which like the lamps and the hand-stencilled ceiling patterns was of traditional Indian design, supplemented the air-conditioning. Each cabin also had a small dressing table with drawers, and an additional elevated bunk

that was ideal for storing luggage. The fittings on *The Royal Orient Express* were not only attractive and sometimes exotically quaint but also surprisingly practical. For example, there were individual lights everywhere and power points offering both 220 and 110 voltage. Each carriage also had a small lounge complete with TV and video player. In addition to this, the library in the bar car had a wide range of books and videos for the passengers' enjoyment. Two large communal bathrooms located at the centre of each carriage, though clean and large, were more problematic – the toilets were fine, but one needed a PhD in engineering to get the showers right! Lined with polished, beautifully carved wood panelling, the dining cars were also authentic, although meals are now partly European and partly traditional Indian. Diligent chefs kept the stainless steel kitchens spotlessly clean and would spend much time between meals preparing the fresh ingredients that were taken on board daily. The bar car was a haven of tranquillity when our train was winding its way from town to town, and was the setting for occasional live entertainment.

We awoke very early the next morning, just as our train

ABOVE: *A crowd of 200,000 worshippers gathers to attend the annual Shiva Festival in Junagadh.*
OPPOSITE: *A curious guard looks out of a beautifully carved window of the fort at Jaipur, the final destination of this luxurious old Raj-style steam-driven tour of the pick of the great sights of Western India.*

was pulling into Chittaurgarh Station. Bleary-eyed we pressed the bell, and were brought the most marvellous strong tea and toast. An hour later we had showered, dressed, breakfasted and were on the bus which was to take us to the fort which had protected this region in past centuries. As we crested a hill, its ghostly shape loomed up in the early morning haze, a distant rooster breaking the silence with a shrill crowing.

Chittaurgarh Fort has a history that is both romantic and tragic. Situated right on the demarcation line between Hindu and Moslem India, the Maharajahs in this area were constantly caught up in fighting the opposing side and, if defeated, could expect no mercy. In 1568, the last of nearly 200 years of battles resulted in the destruction of the fort and palace by the Mughals. In this last battle, 8000 Hindu soldiers, seeing that their cause was hopeless, donned orange robes and marched or rode out of the fort to certain death at the hands of the attackers. In the meantime the women bathed, dipped their hands in henna and put handprints on the wall adjacent to the fort's gate to signify their fate. Then, dressed in their finest silks, they climbed the funeral pyre that had been prepared and, setting it alight, jumped into the flames rather than face rape and dishonour from the attackers. The fort has been abandoned ever since.

We travelled on to Udaipur. Boarding a boat at the jetty, we first passed the town steps where people come to bathe, do their laundry, and enjoy a social chat in a riot of colour and activity. Our boat headed to the famous 'Floating Palace' in the middle of the lake; built on the shallow lakebed, its visual image makes a picture so beautiful that it appears on a large proportion of all posters advertising India. Located on an island in a man-made lake, this edifice best represents the classic image that foreigners conjure up when they think of India, and is arguably the most popular tourist attraction after the Taj Mahal. Today it is a five-star hotel.

Back to the jetty and soon we were visiting the 17th-century Palace of the Maharajah of Udaipur. Two wings of this palace now serve as a hotel, the third as a museum. Among

LEFT: *With lots of steam and hissing, the colourfully decorated locomotive of* The Royal Orient Express *arrives to collect its next group of privileged passengers waiting eagerly at the station in Delhi.*

the displays are photographs of the tiger-shoots enjoyed by the then-Maharajah, who once bagged 33 tigers during one hunt; their mounted heads leered at us from almost every room. The only tigers now found in this area decorate palace walls.

From the windows of the upper floor museum, we could see four large oval indentations in the courtyard. This was where the ruler's elephants were washed down each day. Today, the Maharajah can no longer afford to keep elephants, and must restrict himself to five Rolls Royce, eight Mercedes and a Jaguar. As we departed the Palace we spotted the current Maharajah, a small portly figure with a huge handlebar moustache, supervising the delivery of some new furniture. We were tempted to question him as to the number of his wives – one of his predecessors had one thousand, all confined to the Palace grounds.

The next morning, as our train chugged across the Indian plain towards Junagadh, we were invited to sit in the Lounge Car. Here, an internationally famous 72-year-old Indian puppeteer had set up a fabulous show. As his 11-year-old grandson accompanied him on the drums, he brought the puppets to life as he chanted tales of ancient kings and magical adventures. The entire experience was unique and totally charming.

Our train pulled into Junagadh as the Shiva Festival was

starting. A giggle of attractive Indian girls, sent by the local tourist board, flashed captivating smiles as they presented us with flower bouquets and sweet-smelling frangipani necklaces, marking our foreheads with the traditional red dot. Boarding our bus, we went into town to join the throng of 200,000 individuals who had also arrived for the Festival. Some were in clearly expensive suits and magnificently embroidered and colourful saris, while others were in beggars' rags and it was interesting to note that there was no animosity or friction between the two groups, who mingled freely on their way to the temples.

We headed for the large rock on which Emperor Ashoka had his Buddhist edicts engraved 2400 years ago. The messages exhort citizens to 'purity of thought, gratitude, deeds of kindness, honesty, liberality, meditation and the planting of trees along the highways' – not a bad code to live by! Back to the train and on to Veraval where the famous Somnath Shiva Temple stands right on the edge of the Arabian Sea. Legend has it that the first temple was so rich that it was built entirely of gold and employed 300 musicians, 500 dancing girls and 300 barbers who shaved the heads of visiting pilgrims. This

ABOVE: *The plush interiors of* The Royal Orient Express *recall the glory days of rail travel in India, when the Maharajas travelled in style.*

day it was crowded wall-to-wall with worshippers.

The Gir National Reserve, near Devalia, was another surprise. Most people only associate lions with Africa. Not surprising, when one considers that the Indian lion, also known as the Asian lion, was almost hunted to extinction. By the 1920s only 30 of these magnificent beasts were left in the whole of Asia. Fortunately, an enlightened Maharajah created the Gir National Reserve in 1913, where rare Indian wildlife like these lions and Asian leopards add to the local deer, crocodiles and other species generally associated with Africa. The recorded number of lions has grown to 304, with a breeding programme that allows for surplus cubs to be shipped to zoos and offshore breeding areas.

From the Gir Reserve our train headed for Diu. Once a Portuguese colony, this land was forcibly acquired by Mrs Gandhi's troops at the same time that Goa was 'liberated' by India. The eight churches that existed during the Portuguese rule are now reduced to one whose Indian Catholic priest we met during our visit. Now that the Portuguese families have returned to Europe and there is no more European trading, Diu has reverted to being a small unobtrusive fishing port. Despite the lack of international trade, Diu has one of the highest literacy rates in the district and some of the highest income in India. In the adjacent town of Ahmedpur, we dined at a romantic open-air restaurant overlooking the Arabian Sea. Our sumptuous meal could not have compared, however, to the feast the local mosquitoes enjoyed at our expense.

Following an early breakfast, we boarded our ever-present Gujarat tourism bus and headed for Palitana, a sizeable town that was in a festive mood. Palitana is to followers of the Jain religion what the Vatican City is to Catholics. It has many temples and shrines to Moslem and Hindus, and we were fortunate to get there on a holy day when huge crowds were coming to the hilltop temples to pray. The bus dropped us at the demarcation edge between a vast plain and the towering face of Shertrunjaya. From the base of the mountain a pathway snaked up and up – and further still – to the clusters of temples at the summit. What we could see of the path was only a tiny fraction, the total amounting to 3572 steps that rose up, reminiscent of Jack's beanstalk, and reached into the clouds. It is said that there are 863 Jain temples in the complex, and as this was a major Jain holiday, thousands of worshippers, dressed in their festive best, were puffing up the gruelling four-hour mountain trek.

For the foreign, the feeble and the frail, there are teams

ABOVE LEFT: *This red-turbaned guard at the Jaipur Palace is proud of his snowy-white curling moustache and was happy to pose for a photograph.*
ABOVE RIGHT: *Viewed from the Fort at Jaipur, the blue-roofed new suburbs of the city are seen spreading into the hills.*

of carriers that, often puffing on ganja (marijuana) cigarettes, will carry the person up on a beach chair lashed onto two bamboo poles. The porters heave and sweat their way to the top, taking anywhere between 90 minutes and two hours. The summit, at 457 metres (1500 feet), offers a marvellous panoramic view of the entire plain and town spread out in a tableaux below.

The main Jain temple intrigued us – surrounded by intricately carved ceilings, columns and marble floors, images of the Jain God looked like snow-white figures of Buddha. Young male and female assistants carried rose petals, roses and a mixture of turmeric and what looked like honey, giving these to worshippers for offerings to Jain. The journey down was much faster; at a semi-jog it took only 40 minutes. Back on the train we headed for Sarkhej where we arrived in time for dinner, and were welcomed at the station with flowers and an off-key fanfare blasted by a local trumpeter. We dined at Vishala village, Sarkhej's premier tourist attraction, a vast vegetarian restaurant complex highly popular with both locals and tourists. It features a museum of Indian cooking utensils, an Indian floorshow and local-style cuisine. Diners sit on the floor and eat finger food from dried lotus leaves stitched together to form a mat. Everyone in Gujarat seems to wear turbans; the only other Indians who do so as frequently are the Sikhs.

A short bus ride deposited us at Ahmedabad, where our train awaited, and we settled into our welcoming compartment for a well-deserved night's sleep. The following day we visited the town's Stepwell. A Maharajah built this well that goes five floors underground, so that he would have a place to keep cool in the 40°C (104°F) summer heat. The Gandhi Ashram Museum, where Gandhi lived and preached non-violence after his return from South Africa, is also located in Ahmedabad and the home and school of the father of modern, independent India has become a national shrine.

From here we moved on to the Calico Museum. Designed by Le Corbusier, the building houses arguably the finest textile museum in the world. The landscaped gardens are interspersed with beautifully restored merchants' houses of the 1800s built in classic Indian style and heavily decorated with carvings and fresco-like paintings. Here the most interesting heritage of India's textiles is beautifully displayed.

By morning we had arrived at Jaipur, sadly marking the end of our incredible journey. We headed for the famous Observatory, where great outdoor instruments half relying on the sun and half on the moon for their accuracy, included a clock sundial accurate to within three seconds. Then on to the Jaipur Palace, where handsome handle-bar-mustached Palace guards posed for tourist photos when officials were out of sight. All too soon it was time to bid our fellow passengers farewell, exchange addresses and wave goodbye to the train and crew that had looked after us so well.

ABOVE: *Bathing in the man-made lake and washing brilliantly coloured saris is a social and community affair on the town steps of Udaipur. Across the water lies the famous and beautiful 'Floating Palace', now a five-star hotel, which is actually built on the shallow bed of the lake.*

The Eastern & Oriental Express

SINGAPORE TO BANGKOK

by Gary Buchanan

THE GRANITE FRIEZE OF ANGLO-SAXON musclemen posing as 'Agriculture', 'Commerce', 'Industry' and 'Transport' above the portico to Singapore's Keppel Road Station was my first encounter with the surreal experience that lay ahead. Uniformed attendants whisked me and my luggage to the reception desk inside the pillared art deco amphitheatre of the main station, where pretty girls in kebaya sarongs smiled a welcome. A few minutes later, I was escorted to the most comfortable train east of Eden, where a silk-jacketed steward bowed graciously before inviting me to board.

Racing-green and ivory, twisting and curling like a serpent, the *Eastern & Oriental Express* began its advance north from the high rise, high tech 'Lion City'. Sprawling housing estates gave way to the airport-style Woodlands Station where formalities were completed and we officially left the Island Republic. As the 22 carriages crossed the Johor Causeway, linking Singapore with Malaysia, drivers in motorcars on the adjacent roadway stared at the train, shimmering in an afternoon heat haze. Johor Bahru Station, on the northern shore, is quaintly colonial, with fancy ironwork and neat potted plants – the crescent and star on the coat of arms above the station entrance a reminder that I was now travelling in a muslim country. When afternoon tea was served in the privacy of my sleeping car, the Thai steward explained how to operate the air-conditioning and light controls; the clever tilt of the Venetian blinds and the temperature controls in the shower. Earl Grey was daintily poured from a silver teapot, while outside the southern tip of the Malay Peninsula reaffirmed, if I had any doubt, that I was journeying deep into the tropical jungle.

Coffee trees, small, round and dark green with white flowers and bright red beans; cocoa trees with large droopy leaves and fat pods hanging underneath; rubber trees, growing in monotonous ruler-straight rows, tall and straggly with blotchy grey-white trunks and black slashes where they have been tapped. Vegetable gardens, banana trees, date palms and mangy, long-eared cattle heralded small villages with houses built on stilts and ladders that reached up to their doors; but all around the steamy-hot, impregnable green jungle reigned supreme.

As the tropical twilight gave way to a dark star-studded sky, I considered the options of where to dine – the Chinese-lacquered Singapura Restaurant car, or the elm-panelled Siam dining car? In each, the atmosphere of understated elegance enhanced the exotic flavours of Europe and Asia. Later, ensconced in the bar car, complete with Thai wall carvings, marquetry and engraved mirrors reflecting the soft-peach

---

ABOVE: *Dessert, 'baked samoosa of fruits with ginger ice cream', served after lunch on the* Eastern & Oriental.

RIGHT: *The appropriately exotic logo of the* Eastern & Oriental Express *decorates the racing-green and ivory exterior of the dining car.*

cushioned upholstery, brass fittings and Pullman-style lamps, I watched our arrival into Kuala Lumpur station accompanied by Broadway melodies performed by the resident pianist. This is certainly the grandest station in Southeast Asia, complete with onion-domed cupolas and minarets, Moorish arches and spires. Retiring just before midnight I watched the mighty Petronas Towers light up the night sky as we departed the Malaysian capital. My pillow had been adorned with a Thai wreath of jasmine, but it was the hypnotic motion of the train negotiating the metre-gauge tracks, in tandem with a single malt 'for the rails', that ensured a good night's sleep.

Three types of sleeping accommodation are available on the *Eastern & Oriental Express*, and all have a toilet and shower room en suite. Pullman compartments are similar in size to the classic 'wagons-lits' of Europe, while the state compartments are twice as large and have two lower beds. There are also two commodious Presidential Suites.

Dawn broke and the overnight journey receded as the train arrived at Ipoh. Here, at the self-styled 'Tin Capital of the World', a few bungalows close to the station, with latticed verandas, created the illusion of a Malaysian outstation – with its club, rest-house and rubber estates.

From the open opera observation car I viewed the early morning mists clinging to the forest as the opalescent light revealed oddly shaped, pale-pink and red limestone cliffs, and outcrops with terraced hillsides, and rivers that sparkled in stony beds. These scenes were in stark contrast to the muddy jungle rivers of the previous day. From my vantage point on the open deck I photographed the front of the train as it climbed slowly on the twisting tracks, high above steep gorges into which several rubber trees had escaped to become forest giants.

As the *Eastern & Oriental* continued north, saffron-robed monks and spirit houses began to appear – a sign that Buddhism and animist Thailand was approaching. By the time the rest of the passengers had finished a light breakfast in their compartments, the train descended to the classic Southeast Asian scene – emerald-green rice paddies stretching to the horizon, dotted with tiny thatched houses on stilts and farm-hands in cone-shaped hats cajoling water buffalo into work.

At 09:00 we arrived at Butterworth. Traditionally the terminus for the southbound journey from Thailand and north from Singapore on regular railway services, this modern station is the mainland connection point for the spice island of Penang. From here guests take a break from railborne cosseting with a two-hour excursion to George Town. I was fascinated by the colonial history of the town, and its busy waterfront with markets selling a vast array of Chinese, Indian and Thai goods, but declined to visit the Snake Temple – where, I was told, live snakes nestled on the altar.

Departing just before lunch, the *Eastern & Oriental Express* sped towards Thailand. At the border crossing, Padang Besar, the hostesses in the bar and observation cars miraculously reappeared in golden Thai costumes and proffered Thailand's Singha Gold beer in preference to Singapore's Tiger beer. Clocks were retarded one hour as my dutiful cabin steward attended to passport formalities.

The 'Express of Excess' was now travelling through former Siam. Winged-roof Buddhist temples replaced domed Islamic mosques. At Hat Yai, the train was mobbed by hawkers selling fruit and cooked chickens from vast plates, made from woven palm leaves, balanced precariously on their heads.

As I prepared to enjoy my second night on board, I washed away the remnants of the day in my private shower. Joining fellow revellers, I debated whether to opt for the Fillet of

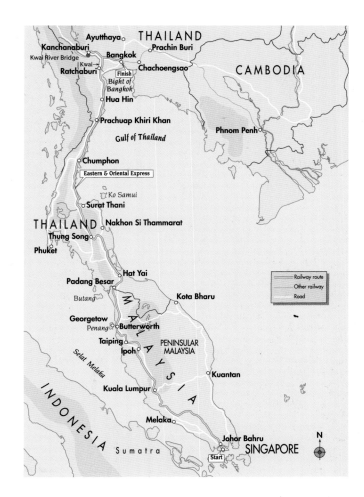

Szechwan-style beef or the rraditional Malaysian spicy fish curry. Newly-made acquaintances convened for drinks in the bar car or casually discussed great journeys of the world in the Burmese teak surroundings of the elegant Pullman Lounge, complete with its library and boutique.

Early the following morning the train passed the classical image of Thailand's hinterland: straw-hatted men wading chest-deep through canals harvesting exotic flowers, naked children playing in the shallows, and white egrets winging their way over lime-green paddies. As the warming sun rose yet higher in the sky, steam rose from the water-logged fields to create a surreal haze.

OPPOSITE: *A hostess proffers drinks in the luxurious interior of the train's bar car, richly decorated with Thai wall carvings and marquetry.*

The final leg of this 42-hour jungle adventure, travelling 2020 kilometres (1255 miles) through the Malay Peninsula, saw the train take a branch line westwards to Kanchanaburi for a visit to the picturesque River Kwai. The dramatic Burmese mountain backdrop belies its grim reputation in World War II as the scene of the Death Railway. We disembarked here, and after photographing our train making its way across the 'Bridge on the River Kwai' we enjoyed an hour-long bamboo raft trip down the river itself, where we observed raft houses moored along the banks amidst tropical vegetation, before returning to the train.

A few hours later, the *Eastern & Oriental Express* skirted the outlying villages of Bangkok where hawkers had set up their mobile kitchens so close to the railway tracks that they were in danger of being run over; the imperturbable Thais squatted on the edge of the line enjoying their second rice meal of the day. Inside our gleaming, air-conditioned carriages I savoured my own lunch, watching villagers and traders preparing their market wares – peeling and carving pineapples, shaving coconuts and dissecting water-melons.

ABOVE: *The Thai 'sales maiden' for the onboard* Eastern & Oriental *boutique shows off an E&O logo kerchief.*
RIGHT: *The* Eastern & Oriental Express *halted at Butterworth Station, the mainland connection point for the Malaysian spice island of Penang.*

All too soon the elegant calm of this oriental odyssey was abruptly shattered as Bangkok's Hualamphong Station, a busy metropolis of travellers and khaki-uniformed officials, bid a noisy, frenetic welcome to the posh travellers. I had arrived at my destination and it signalled the end of a tropical railway adventure slightly removed from reality. The *zeitgeist* of the train was perpetuated in this potpourri of a city, which blends the ancient and the modern unlike any other in the world.

ABOVE: *A cacophony of noises, colours and smells typifies Bangkok's Chinatown. All day long its residents are busy buying and selling, shouting, playing* mah jong, *drinking tea and eating. It is a montage of oriental lifestyles.*
LEFT: *The 22-carriage-long* Eastern & Oriental Express *snakes its way along through lush tropical vegetation in Thailand.*

China Into Vietnam

BEIJING TO HANOI

by Peter Neville-Hadley

THE JOURNEY OF NEARLY 3000 KILO-METRES (1860 miles) from Beijing to Hanoi must begin with the single step of buying a ticket, but it is one of the hardest steps to take. Beijing Station does not have international railway tickets. The international railway ticket office, tucked away inside a hotel, has tickets for Ulaan Baatar, Moscow, and even for Pyongyang, but none for Hanoi.

Tickets to Hanoi must be bought inside a particular branch of the Construction Bank of China, so it is not surprising that few foreigners find them. The railway information line tells you this, but only in Mandarin, and it takes a visit to the foreigners' ticket office at the West Station to obtain directions to the bank. Across an ill-lit marble-floored banking hall is a screened-off corner acting as a travel agency adorned with adhesive characters saying *Henei*, the Chinese name for Hanoi.

There is no one there, but there is a piece of paper taped to the interior of the glass, which in spidery, handwritten characters gives the mobile phone numbers of agency staff.

ABOVE: *The Chinese rail carriages which host the 2967-kilometre (1854-mile) railway journey from Beijing to Hanoi are certainly not luxurious, but provide a window on daily life in China.*
RIGHT: *Vendors sell food on railway platforms to the hungry throngs of passengers. Here travellers buy Zhutongfan – sticky rice baked in bamboo tubes – on the station at Guilin North.*

A telephone call confirms the details, and after providing a passport number the booking is accepted. Next day, two middle-aged women are sitting behind the glass unhurriedly counting large bundles of cash, a process one of them eventually interrupts in order to fill out an international ticket form with values in Swiss francs.

'It's strange' I say, 'that tickets to Hanoi are only on sale here.'

'Yes,' she smiles, 'very strange.'

'Why aren't they on sale at the International Ticket Office?'

'Because we don't give them any.'

And that's all the explanation I'm going to get.

News of China's plan to spend US$12-billion on a high-speed *maglev* (magnetic levitation) line between Beijing and Shanghai may give a false impression to the prospective traveller. Indeed, the uncertain glitz of China's major cities belies the truth of what remains predominantly a third-world country, and the reality of rail travel is that it is mostly rattletrap. It is functional and not romantic, but it is the best way to get around, showing you the authentic and predominantly rural China, and bringing you face to face with ordinary Chinese.

Beijing itself is often a disappointment to visitors, although that's mostly the fault of their own unrealistic expectations. This city of traffic jams and 24-hour, seven-day construction is a reflection of modern China's slow transformation into a 'socialist market economy', and as 'real' as it gets. The picturesque remnants of courtyard houses are rapidly being demolished, including a large area flattened for the construction of the new West Station. One of the most impressive and most vulgar buildings in Beijing, it is a postmodern assemblage of popular motifs from China's architectural past, with hints of arrow tower and Forbidden City all

trains in China, but this is really just an everyday epic – a domestic train in disguise. Four comfy beds in two tiers are adorned with lacy fringes and antimacassars, matching the cloth on the tiny table. Beneath this a garish thermos flask contains piping hot drinking water from the boiler at the end of the carriage, used for making tea and *fangbian mian* – instant noodles.

At 10:51, whistles blown and doors slammed, we depart with a sudden jerk and a sway of the net curtains. Clearing Beijing's sprawling suburbs takes some time, but subsequent cities, hours apart, are minor interruptions in the long trek across the brown and green North China plain, chequered with miniature fields. Grain is laid out on roads to be threshed by passing traffic. Fields of beheaded maize form scale-model forests, later to be used as cattle fodder, the heads drying in bright splashes of yellow on the roofs of brick courtyard houses shrouded in trees against the summer sun. The walls alongside the line, once painted with slogans such as 'Use Mao Zedong thought to arm our minds' still carry the odd injunction – 'Only give birth to one' – but mostly reflect the rise of consumerism, carrying advertising for fertilizer, medicines, hair dye and televisions.

China is perhaps the last great railway-building nation.

out of scale, both with each other and with a vast arch in the centre.

Given the size of China and the nature of its terrain most railway journeys are epic, and have three classes: hard seat, hard sleeper, and soft sleeper. Train T5 runs daily to Nanning in the southwest, but twice a week carries two extra soft sleeper carriages that continue to Vietnam. Passengers have their own armchair-crammed waiting room, and separate access to the platforms, largely avoiding the masses struggling for the few unreserved places in the hard seat section. International trains tend to be a little more upmarket than domestic

---

ABOVE: *The dining car on Train T5 to Nanning is generally crowded and smoky in the evening, and the food is less than appetizing.*
OPPOSITE: *The post-modern edifice of Beijing's enormous West Station, a hotchpotch of traditional Chinese architectural styles. Although this is the departure point for the journey to Hanoi, tickets could only be bought at a nearby bank.*

The five-year plan which ended in 2000 called for 10,000 kilometres (6200 miles) of new line, some of this doubling track laid down by foreigners nearly a century ago, but brand new routes were also pushed into some of the country's poorest provinces, including one punched through the mountainous heart of Muslim-dominated Ningxia, and another more than 1000 kilometres (620 miles) around the edge of the country's most fearsome desert, the Xinjiang region's Taklamakan (meaning 'go in and you won't come out'). It's no accident, however, that these lines lead to areas with potential for unrest and 'splittism'.

As with the line south from Beijing, much of the system is electrified, with a computerized signalling system. But this enthusiasm for *tie lu*, 'iron road', came late. The British demonstrated a small model engine in Beijing in 1865 and later built the first railway station within Beijing's walls (which has recently reopened as a shopping centre). The first proper line, however, was built by the French in Shanghai, bought by the Chinese government, and promptly torn up. Nevertheless, between 1896 and 1905 foreign powers built more than 10,000 kilometres (6200 miles) of track, forming the base of the modern system. Finally, in 1909, American educated Zhan Tianyou built the first all-Chinese line, which tunnels under the Great Wall at Badaling.

As the train trundles steadily south, the scenery becomes repetitive. Pomegranate orchards, their trees hung with neon fruit, are followed by ugly industrial areas of hideous cement walls and stacked dormitory accommodation, then more fields and trees. By early afternoon a dusk-like gloom has set in, through which it is barely possible to see to the edge of the nearest field. Spiralling columns of smoke from burning mounds of stubble seem the obvious cause, but the effect is year-round. We cross the occasional broad and dry riverbed, their banks rising several metres above the surrounding fields. At about 17:00, more than 600 kilometres (370 miles) from the capital, we spend a full minute crossing the Yellow River, traditionally the cradle of Chinese civilization. Now over-dammed and over-drained, it fails to reach the sea for much of the year and in early autumn, it is barely a trickle. Most of the passengers in the Hanoi carriages are Vietnamese, and by now, most of them are asleep, undisturbed by the occasional trolleys bearing *kuai can*, 'fast food' in cardboard boxes, their arrival announced well in advance by attendants with voices of steel. The staff are bored, and happy to chat, coming in and nearly sitting on a

slumbering Vietnamese body, which fails even to stir. They're from Nanning, which for most of the train is the terminus, and they have filled their tiny compartment at the end of the carriage with goods to sell at home.

That evening the restaurant car is packed, its opposite end barely visible through clouds of smoke and a line of peasants from the hard sleeper carriages beyond, filling the space

ABOVE: *Passengers make their own informal way on and off a local train at Dong Dang railway station on the border of Vietnam.*
OPPOSITE: *A vendor wearing a characteristic Vietnamese conical straw hat keeps herself busy while she waits for customers to buy her traditional wares in the railway station in Hanoi.*

between tables. When a seat finally appears the waiter, wearing a police uniform and clutching a scrap of paper with a list of six overpriced dishes in scribbled characters, sits down too while he takes the order. The result, a plate of bony chicken scraps, another of beans swimming in oil, both already cool, brings one of Mao Zedong's sayings to mind: 'You can't have a revolution without hot food.' Although the Chairman was referring to spiciness rather than temperature, the congealed mess on the plates, next to rice of dentine-threatening hardness, produces a revolution in my stomach, and hungry peasants waiting for any sign that I might move on, are only too happy to take my place.

Hankou stands on what the Chinese call the Chang Jiang, or 'long river', and foreigners call the Yangtze. In contrast to the arid early autumn chill of Beijing, left 1205 kilometres (748 miles) to the north, the night air is pleasantly warm and moist. Traditionally, but in defiance of common sense and simple observation, life is very different on opposite sides of the river. It supposedly snows north of the Yangtze but not south, and rice is supposed to be grown south of the river, but wheat to the north. The river also marked a break in the original foreigner-built railway. 'New' China was an imitator of the cement- and steel-obsessed Soviet colossus, and throwing the first bridge across the Yangtze, a monster with both a road and a rail deck, was a symbol of a China which Mao claimed in his 'Great Leap Forward' campaign would overtake the West in only a few years. Once austere, its towers are now outlined with lights, and its banks lined with neon-lit floating restaurants.

In the morning, the view is of neatly terraced rice fields with water supplies carefully husbanded in tiny channels. Rice stalks stand bound in bundles or built into miniature ricks while elsewhere, shimmering green new crops and plump plants wait to be harvested. Partly submerged nets indicate that the flooded fields are also used for breeding fish.

By mid-morning of the next day the countryside begins to grow the spines of some of China's most famous scenery – the karst limestone peaks around Guilin, subject of endless galleries of traditional Chinese painting. Here visitors drift down the river between hills christened for animals and objects to which they bear an uncanny dissimilarity, and watch men fishing from bamboo rafts using trained cormorants. Hundreds swarm off the hard sleeper and hard seat sections of the train to be attacked by map sellers and tour guides, and harried by over-amplified announcements and electronic signs. A search of the platform for food, often a better and certainly cheaper alternative to the dining car, yields *zhutongfan* – rice with bits of sausage served in a fat bamboo tube with a hinged flap in its side for access: greasy and chewy, but palatable.

South of Guilin the train, now diesel, ambles past peasants doubled up over their crops, and banana palms, the first sign of the tropics. The train tires of winding round the peaks and bores through some of them, running past villages with walls of yellow brick enclosing houses screened by stands of bamboo. The scenery levels out again, and as the afternoon progresses, peasants are seen riding home on water buffalo between fields of sugar cane and an ever-diversifying variety of palms. In the late afternoon an attendant comes to us. At

Nanning, he explains, the train will stop for three hours to be dismembered, the two soft sleeper carriages being extracted from the middle of the train, and attached to a few new hard sleepers for passengers joining the train. From then on there will be no dining car until the Vietnamese side, but passengers can leave the station and go for dinner in town.

One benefit of travel in 'soft sleeper' class is that you can turn off the public address system, which is compulsory listening throughout the remainder of the train. However, as we approach Nanning I switch it on just in case there's any useful information. The introduction gives the year in which Nanning was 'liberated', lists the products made there, and remarks that the junctions do not have traffic lights, which

I discover to be false almost immediately upon walking out of the station. The broadcast should have said that the populace behaves as if the crossroads do not have traffic lights. Nanning is known as 'the green pearl,' although the only way you can distinguish it from most other Chinese cities is the presence of palm trees. Its population is two million, but there are few lights, and surprisingly few places to eat near the station. From Nanning the now much shorter train trundles off into the darkness, arriving at the Chinese border just after midnight. Crossing between two of the last nominally communist countries ought to produce a little drama but a group of distinctly unthreatening men and women in mush-

room-coloured military uniforms get on. They are bored, with little to do but stand around and chat, and pass the passports from hand to hand, comprehending very little of what they contain. Three hours of intermittent dozing later, documents returned, the train rumbles gently on across the border to Dong Dang, in Vietnamese territory, where a handful of

passengers sleepwalk off the train, dragging their baggage. The yellow-painted building has a small-scale grandeur with hints of France in louvred windows and in the Vietnamese word for station: ga. The bedraggled travellers sit on wooden benches in one corner near three windows where bored customs and immigration officials, having dealt with the paperwork, sit and do nothing at all. Everyone reluctantly puts their watches back one hour, extending what seems to be an interminable wait.

Dawn breaks slowly on what will clearly be a muggy and clammy day. Eventually invited to board the train, we wander across the tracks to a carriage which seems equipped for civil war, its windows a triple layer of sliding shutters, glass, then mesh screens, all of which can be raised by manipulating awkward bolts. The lower berth in my compartment can be lifted to form a comfortable sofa and hidden beneath the small table is a handbasin with running water. The WC is a French-style squat with footrests. Vietnamese railway lines were built by the French, with a narrower gauge than the European standard, and everything seems slightly scaled down. The presence of no less than three small locomotives at the front of the train suggests that it's going to be a struggle.

The train sets off at walking pace, and as we pass through villages little different in architecture from those on the Chinese side, we are often overtaken by cyclists on ancient Chinese boneshakers, who don't seem to be trying very hard. The dining car has a pleasant old-world woodiness, but there's no one there except three attendants, all knitting, unwilling to provide boiled water, and only slightly interested in selling some coffee. Once the various window layers are manhandled out of the way there are views of people in conical woven hats carrying goods on bamboo poles, and of motorbikes carrying whole families. The rhythmic rattle and clatter through the open window and the purr of an ancient fan is a pleasant change from the sealed environment of the Chinese train. An attendant insists the grille be closed against stone-throwing boys, and later an urchin hurls something, although from too far away to be dangerous. A passenger train seems to be such a rarity that everyone stops work in the fields to watch it pass.

The train clatters over the long misshapen bridge across the muddy waters of the Red River, and finally trundles into Hanoi's railway station, a long yellow colonial building with a bombed-out centre that has been replaced with a hideous concrete structure. A quick change of US$100 makes me an instant millionaire in local currency, and it's off into the two-wheeled traffic jams of millions of motorbikes to find peace, quiet, and a shower at the 1901 elegance of the Hanoi Metropole.

Later, over a *café au lait* with expatriate friends, there's a sense of achievement, if anything amplified by their astonishment that anyone would want to travel in such a slow and inconvenient manner. I try to explain. There may be flights almost everywhere around China now, but travelling by train means a banquet of scenery is brought, course after course, directly to your window, and what could be more convenient than that? Flying reinforces the impression of a modern, urban, internationalized China, while travelling by train gives the traveller a real appreciation of the country's vast size, and reveals the truth of an overwhelmingly rural society, with much of the landscape little changed for hundreds of years, worked by *ku li*, 'bitter labour'.

To see 'real' China and Vietnam, take the train.

OPPOSITE: *A peasant cycles through fields of maize near Long Bien Bridge in Vietnam.*
RIGHT: *The elegant colonial building of Hanoi's main railway station has a modern concrete centre, the result of American bombing.*

AUSTRALASIA

The Ghan

ADELAIDE TO ALICE SPRINGS

by Philip Game

CENTRAL AUSTRALIA AND ALICE SPRINGS LIE at the heart, spiritual and geographic, of the oldest and driest continent. In 1929, having set out from Adelaide, the first train took two days to reach Alice Springs, thus heralding an end to the legendary isolation of the outpost made famous in Neville Shute's *A Town Like Alice*. For decades the central Australian railway, nicknamed 'The Ghan' for the Afghan cameleers who once led their convoys across the Outback, remained a vital but erratic lifeline, the narrow-gauge track often washed away by flash floods or undermined by the shifting sands of the Simpson Desert.

The original Ghan survived until 1980. Today's re-routed standard-gauge service, which Great Southern Railway, a private company, took over from the Australian National Railways in 1997, bears little relation to the hazards and uncertainties or even the location of the original route, which lay 190 kilometres (120 miles) east of the present alignment. Great Southern Railway (GSR) has extended the service south and east to Sydney and Melbourne (and in 2004 north along the new rail line to Darwin on the Timor Sea). Passengers travelling from eastern Australia awake amidst the rolling, fertile Adelaide Hills, then take a three-hour stopover in South Australia's capital city. *The Ghan* then stops only at the crossroads town of Port Augusta before flashing on through the night. It greets the bright desert day near the Northern Territory border and by mid-morning is gliding into Alice Springs, a thriving, confident town of 22,000 people.

Twenty-four shiny steel carriages, emblazoned with the canary-yellow GSR livery, take on passengers in Adelaide. We are served tea and coffee as the 500-metre (1640-foot) string of carriages moves off. On this October afternoon, wheat, barley, rapeseed and sunflowers clothe the rolling downs of South Australia. We flash through one-street towns like Snowtown,

Crystal Brook and Port Germein. Port Pirie's smelter smokestacks loom up ahead, then give way to glimpses of Spencer Gulf, that jagged tear out of the continent whose waters teem with whiting, flounder, flathead – and shark.

Lush pastures give way to saltbush as we near the coast. 'You can taste it in the meat', says a fellow passenger who grew up on one of these struggling farms. We share the lounge car with a clutch of older Australians, indulging themselves in their retirement – some reliving lengthy journeys on rather less comfortable war-time troop trains. An American tour party differentiate themselves as much by their livelier fashion sense as by their accents.

At 18:00 we stop for 30 minutes at Port Augusta. In the fading light the ochre and umber tones of the grand old station, c1910, evoke the outback – as do the Aboriginal children engrossed in play in the forecourt. Local artists have enlivened an expanse of brick by creating a mural which recreates the unloading of the camel trains, the laying of the tracks and the return home of a wounded 'Digger' from World War I.

ABOVE: *Travelling across the sweltering plains of the Red Interior of Australia to Alice Springs, passengers relax in the air conditioned carriages of* The Ghan.
RIGHT: *Historic carriages of the old Ghan train stand derelict on a deserted siding. This train travelled between Alice and the south coast via the now defunct narrow-gauge Central Australian Railway.*

An old-fashioned station bar dishes up Australia's traditional cold beer, mince-meat pies, Cornish pasties and locally-made lamingtons (chocolate-coated sponge cakes) to the throng of travellers. We've definitely parted company with the *café latte* and the *foccaccia* sandwiches of the coastal cities. To the incongruous strains of Jimi Hendrix's version of *All Along the Watchtower* the train moves off, right on time. Dining cars and saloon are bustling now – our three-course dinner is served in three sittings – and the brightly-lit interiors would intrigue any observer left on the platform.

By the time we pass the lone roadhouse at Pimba, it is cast adrift in a sea of inky black, almost lost in the carriage window reflections. We flash past the lights of Woomera, the town built to service a launching site for European rockets. *The Ghan* then strikes north from the Transcontinental Line at Tarcoola. Out there somewhere is the site of the Nurrungar deep-space tracking station, now stripped of its facilities and its top-secret security rating.

The stony desert of northern South Australia, more arid and sparsely populated even than the red ochre country of central Australia, has long been the obvious choice for weapons testing and other hush-hush stuff, sometimes to the detriment of the hapless servicemen as well as the semi-nomadic Aboriginal inhabitants. This lunar landscape conceals most of the world's precious opals, gouged from the earth by hardy individuals who live in underground 'dugouts' in Coober Pedy (from the Aboriginal name *kupa piti*, meaning 'white man's hole'), just east of the line.

We find ourselves waiting until 21:00 to be seated, but the bottle of dry red on the house soothes any lingering tensions. Pumpkin soup with fresh bread rolls is followed by chicken breast or wine-red kangaroo, served rare with roast vegetables. Dessert of brandied fruit or blueberry ice-cream tops off a gourmet meal far removed from the bad old days of railway catering.

Morning: lift the blind and a hot glare floods in. Hot coffee

---

TOP: The Ghan's *NR Class 4000 HP diesel locomotive takes 20 hours to cover the 1555-kilometre (933-mile) journey from Adelaide to Alice.*
OPPOSITE TOP: *A mural in Port Augusta station evokes the pioneering days of rail travel.*

THE OLD GHAN

The year is 1970: The family station wagon limps into Alice Springs. A sturdy enough Australian-built model, it has survived, with difficulty, 1450 kilometres (900 miles) of 'bulldust': corrugations and creek beds on the unmade road up from the coast, and the inevitable detours to the silent stones of Ayers Rock and the Olgas. With orange juice now pumping through its brake hoses the wagon is rather worse for wear. To shortcut the epic journey home, the suffering stalwart is hoisted, laboriously, onto a flat-bed freight car of the old narrow-gauge Central Australian Railway as the family of five takes its places on the padded leather seats of a dog-box compartment. Threading south through the Simpson Desert, a vast tract of red sand dunes, salt lakes and spinifex grass, 'The Ghan' jolts to a halt in Finke, Oodnadatta and William Creek, towns whose populations struggle to reach three digits.

We disembark, bleary-eyed in Maree at four in the morning. Maree was the starting point for the legendary Birdsville and Oodnadatta Tracks along which the Afghans drove their camel trains into the outback until the turn of the century. A few venerable date palms remain as tangible reminders of their presence – and the steel ribbons across the desert recall their stoic endurance.

materializes at my door. Earth roads of a fiery red slash through the spinifex and the scattered desert oaks, the acacias and the casuarinas of the Red Centre. Across the eastern horizon runs the purple tracery of an inland mountainous vein, perhaps the Rodinga Range: these eroded landscapes are as old, as worn down, as any on the planet. Already we have crossed the invisible line into the Northern Territory, and at the 1167-kilometre (725-mile) marker we flash past a whimsical iron man sculpture. It was conceived by the construction workers themselves, to celebrate the laying of the one-millionth concrete sleeper. Solar cell panels wink beside lonely telecommunications repeater stations.

Pools of surface water explain the profusion of ephemeral wild flowers: purple parakeelya, golden honey grevillea and the rosy dock, a wild hop which may have been introduced to Australia from the Afghan cameleers' saddle bags. The Ghan clatters across the wide sandy bed of the Finke, which has flowed only six times in the past hundred years. In Alice, they say you're a local if you've seen the Todd River flow three times; rarely does real water disrupt the town's annual Henley-on-Todd sand regatta which began as a spoof on England's time-honoured Henley-on-the-Thames but has developed a quirky character of its own.

By 9:30 the distant white mussel-shell dishes of the United States' intelligence facility at Pine Gap peep through the casuarinas. A puzzle to the rest of Australia, Pine Gap is no joke to the property developers, real estate agents and storekeepers of Alice Springs, who pocket many, many millions of dollars each year from their secretive but affluent neighbour. Slowing, The Ghan glides past a racetrack towards Heavitree Gap, a notch in the Macdonnell Ranges that forms the southern portal of 'The Alice', Alice Springs. With our speed cut back to walking pace, we ease past rust-red crags peppered with stark white ghost gums. Once through Heavitree Gap, The Ghan quickly reaches Alice Springs Station. Neither the bland station facilities nor the unremarkable suburban streets of this compact town, betray any hint that as late as the 1950s its population numbered a few hundred hardy pioneers.

In February 2004 the long projected railway line between Alice Springs and Darwin, on the Timor Sea, was finally opened to passenger traffic. Following more than 70 years of discussion and three years of construction, The Ghan now runs north a further 1414 kilometres (878 miles), finally linking the continent of Australia's north and south coasts for the first time by rail.

The Indian Pacific

SYDNEY TO PERTH

by Bruce Elder

ONE AND A HALF DAYS OUT FROM SYDNEY, we awoke to one of the strangest and most captivating sights on earth. Making our way up to the *Indian Pacific's* well appointed and comfortable lounge car we looked out of the large windows, as dawn smudged the horizon with a gentle pink glow, and realized that we were, at last, on the great Nullarbor Plain. This is the moment all travellers on the *Indian Pacific* wait for. It is the true *raison d'être* of the journey. An area four times the size of Belgium (as the brochures proudly declare) which is as flat as a tabletop, totally devoid of water and stretches for more than 1000 kilometres (620 miles). Nullarbor is not, as many travellers think, an Aboriginal word, but in fact derived from the Latin term for 'no trees'. It is certainly an appropriate epithet for this flat wasteland. Scrub, yes. Low-lying and hardy desert grasses, yes. But no trees.

But this is to leap ahead. The *Indian Pacific* is, in the manner of the *Trans-Siberian*, one of the world's epic rail journeys. It is an exercise in endurance. A challenge. One of those trips which travellers can, like a badge of honour, wear with pride. Ask those about to embark on the *Indian Pacific* journey why they feel the need to traverse the second-largest dry desert area in the world, and they will answer simply, 'Because it's there.'

The train leaves Sydney's Central Railway Station – a grand old 19th century sandstone edifice at the southern end of the city's central business district – at 14:55 every Saturday and Wednesday. There are three different classes available. Coach Class, with its upright airline-type seats, is reserved for hardened individuals. Holiday Class offers small but comfortable cabins, with beds arranged in a remarkably clever design. First Class, however, remains the best way to enjoy the journey. The luxury fare is steep, but it includes all meals, which rank high on both quality and quantity. Eating on the

Indian Pacific is akin to eating in a top city restaurant with laid-back, friendly Australian service and a varied menu.

These, though, are merely the creature comforts. Equally important are the travelling companions. This is a journey that draws a special breed of adventurers from around the world and the close quarters kept over these three days creates the perfect environment for exchanging stories and making new friends. Finally, the real joy of the journey is the unique scenery – the large windows on the train serving as a screen for the great cinematic documentary that unfolds over 64 hours. And so there is much excitement when the train heads out through the city's western suburbs – first passing through the older inner city and then into the seemingly endless sprawl of homes which extends to the edge of the Blue Mountains. Sydney is located in a vast bowl, flanked by water and mountains. Since World War II the city has stretched in every direction and today, although it has only about one-third of the population, it covers the same area as Los Angeles. Beyond the Sydney basin the train climbs into the Blue Mountains. Early European

---

ABOVE: *The town of Kalgoorlie is known for gracious old country hotels, such as the Federal Hotel with its wide verandas and 19th century charm.*
LEFT: *The sturdy NR Class diesel engine storms its way through the vast flat wastelands of Nullarbor. Twice weekly these powerful engines pull the Indian Pacific 4352 km (2704 miles) across Australia in 64 hours.*

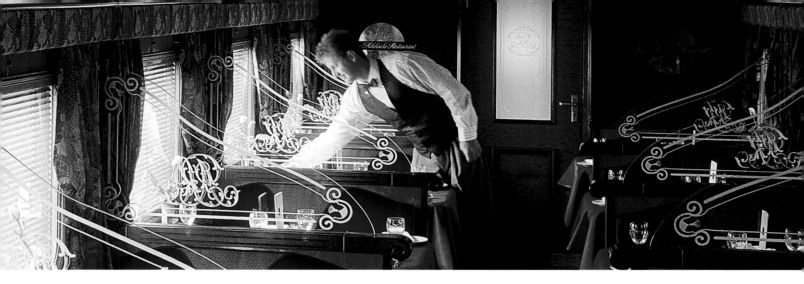

settlers battled to cross the deep gorges and spectacular box canyons of this area, and the train still follows the historic route along the ridges affording occasional glimpses of the gorges. Gracious houses – remnants of a bygone era when the mountains were a hill station to which Sydneysiders escaped from the heat and humidity of summer – can be seen as the train makes its way up Mount Victoria (1092 metres; 3583 feet), before zig-zagging down to the coal mining town of Lithgow. Beyond Lithgow lay the night, and after an excellent meal we retreated to our cabins. The beds were comfortable, the facilities more than adequate and as the rhythm of the train rocked us to sleep, the view out of our window (little more than darkness now) gave no indication of what we could expect in the morning.

Australia from east to west is like a vast and very flat dining table with a slightly crumpled tablecloth pushed up at each end. At the eastern edge, the Great Dividing Range

ABOVE: *The elegant dining room of the Indian Pacific offers excellent cuisine for travellers, who can enjoy the view through the large picture windows while they eat.*

OPPOSITE: *The railway line across the Nullarbor Plain from Port Augusta in South Australia to Kalgoorlie in Western Australia was completed in 1917. The construction, across inhospitable and waterless desert, was difficult and complex, but it was to become a vital part of a national standard gauge network. At the time the service was known as the Trans-Australian Railway.*

(of which the Blue Mountains are part) rises from the Pacific Ocean and slowly drops away through tablelands, sloping to the vast plains of western New South Wales. As the traveller moves further away from the coast the land becomes drier still until, somewhere between Parkes and Broken Hill, it becomes marginal country with low-lying stands of hardy

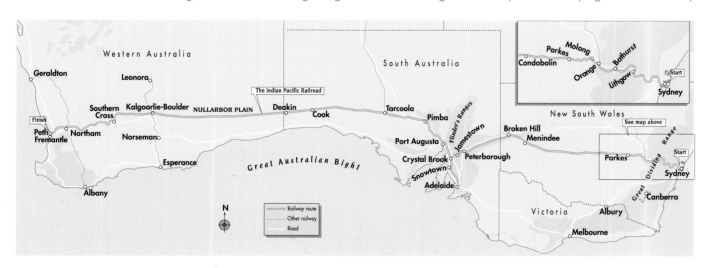

saltbush and spinifex stretching to the horizon. Famous 19th-century writer, Henry Lawson, described this area as 'the great grey plain', and with an average annual rainfall of less than 200 millimetres (8 inches) a year, the sad grey bushes barely survive on the iron-rich and sandy desert soil.

We awoke to a friendly cup of tea brought by the attendant, gazed out the windows and admired the true outback of Australia. It was the beginning of a memorable day. Somewhere to the east of Broken Hill we had moved from the flat, dry outback of western New South Wales through to the undulating hills north of Adelaide, impossibly green and lush in their springtime glory. The contrasting landscape is a perfect example of the illusions created by Australia. In the late 1800s thousands of farmers, seduced by the verdant pastures, moved to this area and built attractive stone houses, confident that they were settling superb grazing country. Less than a decade later drought hit and they were forced to abandon the land. Today the ruins of those proud stone houses stand as a reminder of the harshness and unreliability of inland Australia. Dropping down to Adelaide – the elegant city of churches – the train makes its way back up along the Gulf St Vincent and Spencer Gulf towards Port Augusta, the blue foothills of the Flinders Range visible to the east. Port Augusta, at the apex of the gulf, is virtually the final frontier before the journey west takes us into desert and salt-encrusted lakes spread across the landscape.

The next day brings the full Nullarbor experience. Around lunchtime we stop at the tiny settlement of Cook, 2436 kilometres (1513 miles) from Sydney. To call it a 'settlement' is something of an exaggeration – it is little more than a few sheds among scrubby bushes, out in the middle of nowhere. The train refuels here, so we all climb down from the carriages. Save for a handful of people who cater to the

railway, Cook is now a ghost town. However, there is a monument to a failed scheme to tree the Nullarbor – commencing at Cook with 600 saplings. West of Cook is one of the most celebrated sites in railway lore – the Long Straight. Devoid of any obstacles, the railway charts an arrow-straight path for 478 kilometres (297 miles), the longest straight track in the world. Evening falls before we finally arrive in Kalgoorlie, another mining town, at 22:30. We stay up late into the night with an interesting mix of passengers, sharing thoughts on our cross-continent experience. Time for bed again and by morning the flatness of the Nullarbor has given way to gentle slopes, and the dryness to golden fields and outcrops of gum trees as we approach wheat and sheep country to the east of Perth.

The railway fare from Sydney to Perth is expensive and much of the journey is characterized by unchanging landscape. So why do people embark on the *Indian Pacific*? Perhaps for the opportunity to appreciate the stark beauty of the vast, unyielding expanse that makes up most of Australia. Perhaps because nowhere else on earth can you travel on a train track that is dead straight for a staggering 478 kilometres (297 miles). Most simply perhaps, because it is there.

The TranzAlpine

CHRISTCHURCH TO GREYMOUTH

by Susan Storm

EVEN THOUGH THE ENTIRE JOURNEY is only 227 kilometres (141 miles) long and takes only slightly longer than four hours to complete, and even though the catering features little more than pre-packed sandwiches and tea in polystyrene cups, the TranzAlpine Railway is a transcontinental rail adventure. Traversing spectacular scenery, it is one of the world's great train journeys. The conductor, having travelled the route too many times, jokingly announced at a siding three minutes out of Christchurch that we were privileged to have ridden on the shortest significant train ride in the world and that it was time to disembark. Fortunately, we stayed on board.

The TranzAlpine departs from Christchurch on the Pacific coast of New Zealand's South Island, and runs from the east to the west coast, crossing the Southern Alps and ending at Greymouth. In between, it crosses huge, fertile plains, climbs around geologically complex gorges and twisting river valleys, and traverses a great mountain range by a series of bridges and tunnels that would test the toughest nerves of the agoraphobic and claustrophobic. Then it turns around and goes back again. All in a day's work.

The Southern Alps were well known to the Maori people of New Zealand, as they used the passes to move the spiritually significant and valuable local jade *pounamu* (greenstone) from Arahura and Taramakau in Westland to the region now known as Canterbury. They used the Taramakau-Hurunui route over Harper Pass – a popular route for European travellers to Westland – as it was easiest and had a regular sequence of lakes to replenish food supplies. In the 1850s settlers explored the Canterbury side of the mountains, seeking open grazing land for their sheep. Looking for a quick route to the west coast, a surveyor called Dobson surveyed Arthur's Pass in February 1864 following information about its location given to early explorers by Maori. Dobson's work

became significant when miners discovered gold on the west coast, and needed to quickly find a route to bring their booty to Canterbury.

The road across Arthur's Pass was built rapidly during a very cold winter in 1865, but remained unsuitable for transporting the west coast's economic staples, coal and timber. New Zealand Midland Railway, a private company, began work on linking the west coast with Canterbury in 1887. Midland went broke before the railway was completed and the government took over. Otira Tunnel was the biggest hurdle, taking more than 16 years to construct, but the railway, completed in 1923, soon became a means by which people could travel from Christchurch to go skiing, tramping and climbing. *The TranzAlpine*, which came into existence in 1995, continues to provide a popular link between the west coast and the Canterbury Plains

Clean, efficient, and fast, the journey is underpinned by quirky 'Kiwi' conductors who commentate the trip and divulge snippets of local history and philosophy as the spectacular landscape twists by. Like the oft-related story of

ABOVE: *Passengers relax and strike up conversation on board* The TranzAlpine *as they settle into the four-hour ride across the spectacular scenery of New Zealand's Southern Alps.*
LEFT: *The TranzAlpine crosses the cold Waimakariri River, one of the South Island province of Canterbury's great rivers, and the lifeblood of the local economy.*

RIGHT: *The TranzAlpine crosses New Zealand's Southern Alps from Christchurch on the east coast of South Island to the west coast at Greymouth, stopping briefly at Arthur's Pass, a national park of high mountains with large scree slopes along wide rivers and steep gorges.*

Rosie, the border collie sheepdog who'd come out to meet the passenger train as it pulled into Springfield, and be rewarded with treats of railway pies. Before she died, it was estimated she'd eaten more than 5000.

The TranzAlpine pulls out of Christchurch, often described as the most English city outside England, where pioneers tamed and drained wild swampland to build homes. It passes factories and transport depots, wool sheds and other icons of the country's rich agricultural heritage. The seats in the airy compartments are sparsely settled with a few eager families armed with lunch-stocked eskies (a polystyrene lunch box), and a motley collection of tourists huddled deep into their parkas. The train pulls quietly along the narrow gauge through the beautiful Canterbury Plains, 1.2 million hectares (3 million acres) of intensively farmed verdant fertile soil.

Beyond Springfield, New Zealand's impressive Southern Alps loom into the foreground. There are 185 peaks in the range over 2133 metres (7000 feet) high, and 16 peaks over 3050 metres (10,000 feet). The mountain range has conspired to keep the country geographically divided – and the train edges around the Torlesse Range and into the gorge of the cold Waimakariri – one of Canterbury's great rivers. It is the lifeblood of the local economy, its headwaters rising back near Mount Rolleston and the Browning Pass.

Those who've been sitting complacently staring out of the windows at the pleasantly rolling scenery now race for the back of the train, to the open air observation car. It's filled with shivering tourists and jostling photographers, eager for lasting images of the literally breathtaking scenery. From here, views down the gorge are as thrilling as riding a roller coaster, as it slips in and out of a series of 16

tunnels, five major viaducts – the highest of which crosses over Staircase Creek at 73 metres (240 feet) – and on and off numerous bridges. This open air viewing is not for the faint-hearted, for even in summer there are wild, freezing winds, but it's worth braving the elements to get a bird's eye view of the dramatic landscape. The unending vistas of sheer snow-covered slopes, crumbling hillsides, banks of scree and scoured gullies were caused by colliding tectonic plates in one of the most violent geological conflicts on Earth, where these mountains are still in formation, moving upwards at 2.5 centimetres (an inch) a year.

The TranzAlpine departs from Christchurch on the east coast of New Zealand's South Island and runs to the west coast, crossing the Southern Alps and ending at Greymouth. At the foot of giant snow- and forest-covered mountains; it is a great place to break the journey and discover the diversity of flora and fauna, from eastern beech-clad hills

to tangled rain forest. The highest mountains have glaciers surrounded by tussock basins, flowering herbs and alpine grasses. Beyond Arthur's Pass, the train passes through the 8.5-kilometre (5.3-mile) Otira tunnel, begun in 1907 and completed in 1923, which allowed rail to finally replace the famous Cobb & Co horse-drawn coaches. At a gradient of 1.33 (one unit of elevation per 33 units of distance), the train needs the additional assistance of electricity to pull it up impossibly steep inclines. The train then traverses roaring rivers, skirts podocarp forests, weaves through more mountains and past small gold rush relics, and around Lake Brunner. Finally it follows the course of the Grey River to Greymouth, the west coast's largest town. There you disembark, knowing that in the same time it takes to read the Sunday papers, you have crossed the great divide of New Zealand. Not bad for a morning's sightseeing. Of course, there's always time to go back to Christchurch.

AFRICA

The Blue Train

PRETORIA TO CAPE TOWN

by Susan Storm

THE BLUE TRAIN, THE ICON OF rail travel in South Africa, is advertised as being the most luxurious train in the world. When it took to the tracks again in 1997 for its inaugural run after a radical face-lift that left even its designers gasping, it was indeed a moveable feast. The sequins were out in force. So were the film stars and politicians. As was a media contingent that would make a posse of paparazzi pale in comparison.

The new-look train was officially launched at Pretoria Station by then-South African president Nelson Mandela. Joining him for the launch, followed by one night of serious partying on the train as it sped towards Cape Town, were Archbishop Desmond Tutu, film star Mia Farrow and two of her children, jazz musician Quincy Jones and his biographer James McBride, politician Imran Khan and his then wife Jemima, model Naomi Campbell, Hong Kong actor Tony Leong, Mandela's future wife, Graça Machel, and a select international media group. Amid speeches and dancing, a

riotous crowd jived to the beat of the Soweto String Quartet and raised the rafters with their singing accompaniment. When the new *Blue Train* departed, as all good trains should, exactly on the stroke of ten, thousands of well-wishers on the platform broke into patriotic song.

During the journey from the Jacaranda City of Pretoria, through the desert, and the mountains, and finally to the glistening beaches of Cape Town, revellers reclined in luxury, feasted on game and lobster from monogrammed plates, sipped South Africa's finest wines from crystal goblets, dabbed their mouths with linen napkins and were treated like royalty. Not a speck of dust landed in a mascara'd eye, neither a phone-call nor fax was missed, and not a moment's sleep was disturbed in wide beds under the finest Egyptian linen. And when it arrived in Cape Town 25 hours later, Mr Mandela was beaming. 'It was a wonderful experience... and I was particularly pleased that our journey allowed our honoured foreign friends to get a first hand awareness... not only of the beauty of our land, but of the many remarkable people who have joined hands to form this new nation.'

Train travel has come a long way since the days when the journey – incorporating heat and dust, insects, dubious food and unsavoury travelling companions – took on epic proportions which often overshadowed the thrill of discovery. When a train's list of attributes include cinemascope landscapes from bubbling baths run by personal butlers, who will also iron your evening wear and pop your champagne, when guest lists read like an international *Who's Who*, then a little bit of self-indulgent trumpet blowing is wholly justified. But the prestigious moniker is a real one, extended by the World Travel Awards.

The first people to experience the route now traversed by *The Blue Train* were those who came to the gold and diamond

ABOVE: *No expense has been spared on the train that is the icon of African rail travel. Egyptian linen, silks, crystal, world class food and wine, and spacious compartments ensure a comfortable ride.*

OPPOSITE: *The* Blue Train *travels through vineyards near the Hex River Valley in South Africa's Western Cape Province. It takes two days to complete its 1600-kilometre (994-mile) journey between Pretoria and Cape Town.*

industrial and economic hub of the country 1600 kilometres (995 miles) to the northeast. Electrification took over from steam as the grand all-steel blue icon adapted to progress, and people began riding on *The Blue Train* more for the experience than the journey. After two other refurbishments over the decades to keep up with travellers' needs and technology, *The Blue Trains* underwent their most recent incarnation, incorporating the latest technology with the utmost in interior design.

The spacious compartments have a marble en-suite, with either bath or shower. If guests get withdrawal symptoms from the outside world, there's a telephone, television, CD player and video machine that also screens short documentaries about the area through which the train is travelling. In the Club Car, styled along the lines of a gentleman's club and the ideal place for coffee and a post-prandial drink, a large screen provides a driver's-eye view of the track ahead, via a camera mounted onto the front of the locomotive.

Beyond the luxury and technology, *The Blue Train's* Pretoria to Cape Town route is something to write home about. It is a journey through a plethora of sociological and geographical vistas, from the industrialization of a

fields of South Africa in the middle of the 19th century. A large wagon-building industry developed after the discovery of diamonds at Kimberley around 1880, when travellers to the diamond fields had to transfer from the train to wagons for their difficult trek to the Big Hole. When years later it was decided to continue the rail line from Wellington to Kimberley, the farmer across whose land the line would travel sold his rights on the proviso that the passing trains had always to stop at Wellington. Today *The Blue Train* still upholds this tradition.

Travelling standards improved consistently with the approach of the 1920s, incorporating articulated coaches equipped with heating, hot and cold water, bunk lights and bells to summon the coach attendant. Then came showers and washrooms, electric fans and lighting, oak-panelled dining saloons, smoking and card rooms, luxuries the general public could only dream about. The trains, coloured a distinctive azure, cream and silver, became known as 'those blue trains'.

Synonymous with luxury, and known to be the mode of travel of mining imperialists, they functioned as the premier express between the mail-boats in Cape Town and the

ABOVE: *Nelson Mandela and Graça Machel laughing at Mr Mandela's gaffe at the glittering launch of the new* Blue Train *as it arrived at Cape Town station. He had just deflected questions on terrorism and tourism, and replied 'The train will have a big impact on South Africa terrorism – I mean, tourism!'*

resource-rich city, through barren desert to small towns, across mountain ranges and alongside rivers, through verdant farmlands to end on the Atlantic coast.

The train eases its way towards Johannesburg and its mine dumps, where small children run shrieking along the tracks while the chefs in the stainless steel kitchens dish up smoked marlin from the Indian Ocean, a Cape seafood medley with crayfish and calamari, game fillet and South African cheeses – a feast fit for the crème de la crème of society. Later that afternoon the train stops at Kimberley, seat of South Africa's original diamond rush. This is where Cecil John Rhodes established De Beers, the biggest diamond concern in the world. The scene changes to the dramatic starkness of the Karoo desert, where ostriches lope through dust eddies, the skies erupt into dramatic sunsets, and ancient fossils are testimony to it once being a primeval swamp. Olive Schreiner's quintessential South African novel, *Story of an African Farm*, drew much of her inspiration from this landscape. It is a relief to stretch your legs at historic Matjiesfontein, a tiny, dusty town in the Karoo, where trains used to top up with water and provisions. There's a large, rambling gabled hotel and a teashop, but nothing beats the afternoon tea served in the lounge car on the train.

The Blue Train leaves the barren Karoo when it travels though the Hex River Tunnel system, at 16 kilometres (10 miles) the fourth-longest in the world. It emerges into the fertile Hex River Valley, where lush, colourful vineyards are set against the majestic Matroosberg. Here most of South Africa's table grapes are grown, and in late autumn when the barlinka vines are transformed into crimson, the landscape seems to be on fire. The Hex River is famous for one of South Africa's most romantic and ghostly legends, that of Eliza Meiring, a beautiful young girl, who in 1768 went mad after her beloved fell to his death in the mountains.

The train stops briefly at Worcester then, in keeping with tradition, on to the tiny town of Wellington, before it passes through the wine-growing regions of Stellenbosch and Paarl – founded by Dutch and Huguenot settlers in the late 1600s. Here, just 50 kilometres (30 miles) from bustling Cape Town, quiet avenues of ancient oaks shield whitewashed Dutch gabled homes from the blazing sun. Our journey ends in Cape Town, that beautiful city at the foot of Table Mountain, established over 350 years ago by the Dutch in order to replenish ships passing on the spice route. No longer a halfway harbour, Cape Town's visual beauty of its cliffs, beaches and mountains, is complemented by a lively cosmopolitan atmosphere, hundreds of restaurants and a thriving art community. These attractions combined draw a roaring tourism trade all year round. Now that's a city worth getting off arguably the world's most luxurious train.

ABOVE: *The elegant interior of the Club Car which is styled along the lines of a gentleman's club and is an excellent place for an after-dinner drink.*

The Pride of Africa

---◆---◆---◆---

CAPE TOWN TO DAR ES SALAAM

by Gary Buchanan

NESTLED BENEATH THE LOOMING, distinctively flat-topped massif of Table Mountain, Cape Town enjoys one of the most spectacular settings on earth. This is no sprawling metropolis, but a compact conurbation – a patchwork of modern office towers and red-roofed houses that stretch to the encircling ocean, its thundering surf echoing within the natural amphitheatre created by Table Mountain and the Twelve Apostles. The modern, flat-roofed station seemed an improbable place to embark on one of the world's most entrancing railway journeys, but beside Platform One stood no ordinary train – *The Pride of Africa*, resplendent in bottle-green and ivory livery, evoked the sublimity of a truly grand occasion.

With a cacophony of shrill hoots and purposeful whistles, the 17-carriage train slid out of the station. The electric locomotives slowly negotiated the complex network of tracks and junctions of the suburbs before Table Mountain receded into the distance and the hinterland of Cape Town came into view. In the wine country of Paarl and the Hex River Valley, tangled vines grow in the foothills of starkly chiselled mountains. Modest farmsteads, their white porticoes guarded by cypresses at the end of rutted dirt roads, huddle in sprawling estates. Here and there, guinea fowl scuttle to and fro, among indifferent sheep and horses.

It was late afternoon as the train arrived at Matjiesfontein. We disembarked to visit the historic hamlet, where over 100 years ago Laird Logan set up a small hotel for the hungry, thirsty travellers of the Cape Government Railways. The graceful hotel, named after Lord Milner, provided an opportunity to take the evening air and enjoy a small draught of Castle beer. By the time I reboarded the train, the sun had all but disappeared, leaving a last explosion of light along the earth's rim. The grey earth of the great Karoo was now scarlet, the sky salmon – it was the drunken dusk of the desert.

Ensconced in the observation car, a delicious pinotage in a crystal glass, I watched night creep up on the train. The African bush was in the grip of winter and later, cosseted by an electric blanket and the air-conditioner turned to warm, I fell asleep to the rhythmic, hypnotic motion of the train's wheels.

The following day the train arrived at the fine old Victorian station of Kimberley. This city of diamonds is set in the flat, austere landscape of the Karoo. History was rekindled as I lunched at the Kimberley Club, wistfully recapturing the spirit of the reign of Rhodes, Milner and Jamieson, politicians and mining magnates who clinched so many deals on these premises. The highlight was a visit to the largest man-made hole in the world, appropriately named 'the Big Hole', which had produced 14.5 million carats of diamonds by the time work stopped in 1914.

In the proud tradition of entrepreneurs such as Cecil Rhodes, Rohan Vos has single-handedly created one of South Africa's most romantic travelling idylls. *The Pride of Africa* is an iconoclast and ranks alongside the best of the world's great railway odysseys. Each sleeping car, observation car, lounge

---

ABOVE: *Fine-tuning the regulator of locomotive No. 2702 'Bianca', named after one of Rohan Vos's daughters.*

LEFT: *The 50-year-old workhorse No. 2701 'Brenda' – a mighty Class 19D steam locomotive – was restored at Dunn's Locomotive in Witbank. It now proudly bears the Rovos Rail crest.*

car and restaurant car combines the opulence of pre-war style with subtle modern innovation. Deluxe suites have showers and toilets, and the commodious royal suites have larger lounges and a bath.

Back on the train that night, sequins and sapphires rubbed shoulders with tuxedos and topaz as guests turned out for dinner. A salad of fresh crayfish preceded a saddle of Karoo lamb, accompanied by a copious selection of some of South Africa's finest semillons and sauvignons, chardonnays and cabernets. Inside the cosy restaurant car, with its seven pairs of elegantly carved, roof-supporting pillars and arches, it was high life on the highveld. Beyond the pink curtains, the Free State passed by unnoticed.

Early the next morning, the sun was already gilding the maizelands of the Northwest Province. Approaching Gauteng, the sprawling township of Soweto came into view and a short while later the train settled at Johannesburg's Kempton Park station where we bade farewell to electric traction. Two mighty class 19D locomotives, originally built in 1939, were now in charge. Named after two of Vos's daughters – 'Bianca' in front, 'Brenda' adding further motive power – the steam locomotives wheezed out of the suburban station, leaving commuters behind in a hazy veil of smoke. For an all-too-brief interlude, *The Pride of Africa* looked complete; the evocative panting rhythm and piercing whistles gave voice to the echoes of the past. After a sightseeing tour of the 'Jacaranda City' of Pretoria, administrative capital of South Africa, the train continued east through orange, papaya and avocado groves, past settlements of concrete houses where children ran down to the tracks smiling and waving. In the

observation car the railborne safari had begun in earnest as sightings of impala, kudu and zebra gave me a foretaste of an unforgettable encounter with Africa.

At nearly 20,000 square kilometres (8000 square miles), the Kruger National Park is a game reserve the size of a small country, and we were scheduled to overnight in one of the stylish private reserves along its western edges. Setting out on a sundowner drive that evening, a classic African image composed itself in the tranquil twilight of the bush: a single giraffe, frozen against a crimson sky. The insouciance of the animals somehow separated them from the world, setting them above and apart.

My return to *The Pride of Africa* late the following day was almost an anticlimax as the wild beat of the bush was replaced by the cool elegance of the train. Crossing into Zimbabwe at Beit Bridge, the sun sank peacefully behind curious-looking baobab trees. The cloud of spray above *Musi-oa-tunya*, 'smoke that thunders' (the African name for Victoria Falls) could be seen in the distance the following morning. The screaming of the wheels added to the sense of drama as the train rounded the curve into Victoria Falls Station. The graceful colonial building

ABOVE LEFT: *Observation Car No. 226 'Modder' was the first to be purchased by Rovos Rail and offers a unique platform to experience the majesty of Africa.*

ABOVE RIGHT: *Dating back to the 1920s, dining car 'Shangani' was found in a siding in Natalspruit 1986. Three of the magnificent teak pillars had been removed. After much loving restoration, romance has returned to the rails.*

and imposing hotel alongside are remnants from a bygone era. Liveried hotel staff in white suits and red cummerbunds escorted me from my Edwardian time-piece into yet another blissful haven of elegance.

From the hotel's manicured lawns I could see the great Zambezi plunging across a mile-wide chasm. It was time to relax, savour the remarkable spectacle of sight and sound and contemplate the fact that this pan-African adventure was about to become even more improbable. The next day my train-mates and I would be heading across the mighty iron bridge that spans the Zambezi to follow in the footsteps of David Livingstone.

Spirits were high as we rejoined the train after a hearty breakfast next morning. By now the warm sun shining through the windows of my suite, intensified the dark red-brown mahogany panelled walls. 'Safari' in Swahili means a journey; appropriate then, that this 'Edwardian Safari' should now be taking us away from the tourist trail.

Travelling to somewhere unknown, you never think you'll end up in the place you most feel at home. Yet this is what *The Pride of Africa* had become in a matter of a few days. Somehow the double bed felt even more comfortable, the thick silk bedspread ever more inviting, the soft cushions more reposeful. The writing desk was adorned with new flowers and fresh fruit; the polished woods looked richer; two prints showing South African life in the 1930s gleamed; the shower compartment had been replenished with unguents and the fridge restocked with my favourite tipple.

The train slowed almost immediately. In the observation car frantic fiddling with f-stops, whirring motordrives, buzzing autofocusing and shutters snapping were followed by moments of intense silence and soft sighs as we all gazed in awe at the Victorian bridge spanning the Zambezi. This link, so critical to the expansion of Rhodes's dream of a 'Cape-to-Cairo' railway, was opened in 1905. From the rear vantage point the train appeared to be suspended across the chasm; as if hanging above one of Africa's mightiest rivers.

Our arrival on Zambian railways was signified by the train's reduced speed due to lack of maintenance of the railbed. While narrow by European standards, the 1.06-metre (3½-foot) gauge track offered a surprisingly comfortable ride in South Africa and Zimbabwe, but all that had changed as we lurched, shuddered and wobbled towards our ultimate goal of the Tanzanian port city of Dar es Salaam.

At the former capital of Livingstone the local customs and immigration officials disembarked having enjoyed Rohan Vos's hospitality in the observation car. The entrepreneur has picked up a few persuasive techniques since he began taking his train across national borders; a couple of fine cognacs proved sufficient to oil the wheels of bureaucracy and colour-ful visas miraculously appeared in our passports. Formalities complete, we continued onwards and upwards towards the Batoka Plateau. The land was distinguished only by kilometre after monotonous kilometre of sage bush and occasional acacia trees, which grew like skeletons out of the skin-toned dirt.

ABOVE: *One of the Seven Natural Wonders of the World, Victoria Falls on the Zimbabwe-Zambia border was discovered by David Livingstone in 1855. The bridge spanning the gorge below the falls was completed in 1905.*

The deft service we had enjoyed in the dining car was now replaced by slightly more capricious delivery of both wines and food as the team of waiters and waitresses fought against the vicissitudes of Zambian tracks. Soup became noticeably absent from the menu and fewer guests opted for coffee. My comfortable bed, too, had assumed a personality all of its own; creaking and groaning as the train began to resemble a rollercoaster.

The following morning, earlier than normal thanks to some lively jolts, I opened my shutters to reveal an ochre desert bushscape floating past, sprouting the occasional rocky outcrop or cluster of mud huts. The ponderous rumble of the train wheels was methodically kicking up the dust into the hazy sunrise.

After breakfast I was reminded of that wonderful phrase of Paul Theroux 'I sought trains; I found passengers'. By now this merry band of 62 fellow travellers had become a close-knit community. Train manager, Peter Winterbottom, was as socially adept as he was proficient at administering this moving hotel. We were all on first name terms and social interactions were as varied as the scenery. Some days I would sit in the observation car talking to Ramel and Claudia from Melbourne, Australia; other times I would lunch with Michael and Jocelyn from Beverly Hills, California.

One night I was invited to dine with Rohan and Anthea Vos and became fascinated by their story of how *The Pride of Africa* was created. In 1985 Vos attended an auction at the Railway Preservation Society in Witbank, to the east of Johannesburg. His intention was to acquire an old coach or two, restore them and hitch them to a South African Railways train for family holidays. Several coaches were purchased and taken to the Society's yard to be restored. The difficulties he encountered working with the South African Transport Services soon convinced this charismatic 50-something that he needed his own engine. In December 1986 he found a Class 19D locomotive at a scrap metal yard. Built in 1938, it was recommissioned by Dunn's in Witbank. Eventually permission for Vos to run his train was granted, with the added benefit of a licence for fare-paying passengers. This was when the idea of running a vintage train as a business venture was born. When the authorities vetoed the suggested name of 'Springbok Steam Safaris', it was simply called 'Rovos Rail'. Armed with a history of South African Railways dining cars, Vos started a search for suitable coaches. An early target was the Jewish Guild

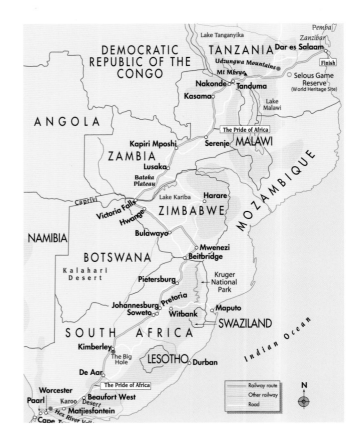

Country Club in Johannesburg where three dining cars were standing, vandalised and dilapidated. They were hauled to Witbank and returned to the rails. Later he bought coach No. 148 'Pafuri', which was originally built in 1911 as an A-17 type dining car. Today the entire Rovos Rail fleet amounts to 75 carriages which run in three separate trains. Inaugurated in 1993, the 12-night 'Edwardian Safari' is an annual highlight in the Rovos Rail calendar, and *The Pride of Africa* that I was travelling on was by now straying far from South Africa on this pan-African extravaganza.

That afternoon, after a short stop at Lusaka station, we continued northwards towards the two separate stations of Kapiri Mposhi. One of the buildings is neglected and silently mocks Rhodes' pretensions of a 'Cape-to-Cairo' railway, which ended here in 1908. The new station, built by the Chinese in 1975, stands clean and secure as a symbol of Red China's attempt at 'fraternal solidarity' with post-colonial Africa. It remains one of the great ironies of Africa that the British imperialist's dream of a railway stretching the length of Africa should have been extended – after the colonial

period had ended – by 1800 kilometres (1120 miles) from Kapiri Mposhi to Dar es Salaam. From the observation car platform I watched the single-track rails of the TANZAM railway disappear into the shimmering haze. Frantic weaver birds darted among the thorn trees while in their shadows hungry goats bleated; howling children were bathed in tin buckets outside daub-and-thatch huts; giggling women at the wheezing water pump waved at the passing train. All around me was the evocative essence of this bright continent: hardwood smoke, hard-work sweat, animal fat and the yawning breath of the hard red earth. I was passing through territory inaccessible by any other means and witnessing a part of Africa unknown to virtually all outsiders.

At the border between Zambia and Tanzania at Nakonde/ Tunduma the on-board historian Nicholas Schofield informed us that we were midway between Africa's two Great Rift Valley lakes. In the cool of the early morning we visited the 64-metre (210 feet) Nkundalila Falls, and later, from the air-conditioned lounge car we watched the domed volcanic peak of Mount Mbeye come into view, signalling our descent

to the Rift Valley itself. Soon the train entered an area of matted creepers and dense jungle. The Udzungwa Mountains forced the train to slow down even further as it negotiated the tunnels, switchbacks and viaducts of the escarpment.

The farewell dinner on board that night was a stylish affair, yet tinged with sadness; this odyssey of 6100 kilometres (3790 miles) was drawing to a conclusion. That night most of us stayed late in the observation car, sipping a few more cognacs than was prudent, our loud voices vanishing into the emptiness beyond the open platform. On the last morning, after traversing the Selous Game Reserve, we entered the chaotic *mêlée* of Dar es Salaam station. The delegation of officials and competing bands provided a fitting crescendo for my journey in time, space and splendour.

ABOVE: *A series of tight curves are a feature of the descent to the Mpumalanga lowveld. Here double-headed steam traction is a railway enthusiast's delight.*

THE AUTHORS

Steve Barry   *Colin Boocock*   *Gary Buchanan*   *Eugeni Casanova*

STEVE BARRY'S life-long interest in trains started when he was growing up in southern New Jersey. Summer evenings were spent with his father Ernie watching the commuter trains coming into his hometown of Millville from the Philadelphia suburb of Camden. Weekends were spent on day trips to the Strasburg Rail Road or riding the Reading's legendary Iron Horse Rambles. Steve started his full-time railfanning after graduating from Rutgers University in 1979. Since then, he has attended every National Railway Historical Society (NRHS) Convention in Washington, DC, as well as every NRHS gathering. He later became the National Director for the NRHS Wilmington, Delaware, Chapter and NRHS Eastern Region Vice President.

Steve has been a contributor to the rail hobby press for about 20 years, starting with an article in *Rail Classics* in 1983. In 1986 he submitted his first article to *Railpace Newsmagazine*, which began a long and productive relationship with the regional news magazine. In 1996 Steve left his vocation of 16 years, accounting, to join the staff

of *Railfan & Railroad* as associate editor. In 1997 he was promoted to managing editor. He'll photograph anything on rails from CSX's latest power to streetcars to tourist steam. He estimates that he has taken about 100,000 slides in 21 years of photography. Steve lives in Newton with his wife Genie, who enjoys riding trains and reads *Railfan* cover to cover every month.

COLIN BOOCOCK has more than 45 years' experience in traction and rolling stock engineering as a career railwayman, and has been a railway enthusiast and traveller all his life. He has developed his hobby to take a keen interest in all types of railways, all types of traction, in the United Kingdom and as many other countries as he can spare the time (and cash) to visit. He has built up a comprehensive collection of photographs and has become a prolific writer of illustrated articles and books (14 railway books to date). His published photographs cover more than 53 years of railways and travel. He still looks to visit new countries and faraway places, choos-

ing train travel wherever possible. 'In a train I am in my most natural and relaxing environment!' he says. He nurtures a wish to embark on a round-the-world journey by train when the time is right.

Born, educated and resident in Scotland, **GARY BUCHANAN'S** affection for trains dates back to his school days, when he commuted across the mighty Forth Railway Bridge to attend college. Since then he has travelled on many of the world's most fascinating railway journeys: crossing Australia on the *Indian Pacific*, enjoying a glimpse of Russian opulence on the *Bolshoi Express*, and venturing into the remote regions of Mexico on board the *Copper Canyon Express*. When the concept of re-creating the *Orient-Express* was mooted in the late 1970s, Gary began researching the history of this famous train. Having taken several journeys on the *Nostalgic Istanbul Orient-Express*, he made sure he was on the inaugural journey of the *Venice Simplon-Orient-Express* in 1982. Since then

Bruce Elder   *Philip Game*   *Jim Gill*   *Walter & Cherie Glaser*

he has travelled on the train more than 50 times and gives frequent television interviews on the train's history. He also enjoys one of the company's other trains, the *Eastern & Oriental Express*, whenever he travels in Southeast Asia. Gary's favourite railway journeys blend re-created opulence from the golden days of travel with the spirit of adventure. To this end he has travelled many times on Rovos Rail's *Pride of Africa* – to Namibia, Zimbabwe, and of course the *Edwardian Safari* to Dar es Salaam. The *Royal Scotsman* offers him a sumptuous platform to explore his own country. He contributes regularly to *The Sunday Times*, *Sunday Express*, *Evening Standard* and *The Herald* in Britain and is regarded as a world expert in the field of luxury railway travel.

EUGENI CASANOVA was born in Catalonia in 1958. He is a journalist and travel writer, but often combines both subjects and turns them into a way of life. As a traveller, he knows all the continents, always moving in local transport and staying with local people. As a journalist, he has exercised all the specialities: the written word, photography, radio, television and the internet. In recent years he has also been a war reporter in the main conflicts, including Bosnia, Kosovo, Algeria, Guatemala, Ruanda, Kurdistan, Western Sahara, Israel-Palestine and the

Sudan. Trains are one of his passions and he has performed a number of the mythical journeys on rails. He accomplished a historical first in completing the longest possible train journey, a Western Europe (Barcelona) to the Sea of Japan (Vladivostok) round trip. He has travelled east via Europe and the *Trans-Siberian*, linking on the way back with the Silk Route, through China and Central Asia. The result of this experience is the book *An Epic Journey: The Trans-Siberian and the Silk Route by Train*. He has also published books about expeditions across the Sahara Desert, the bears of the Pyrenees, and the military campaigns of Medieval Catalonians in the Eastern Mediterranean.

BRUCE ELDER is a senior journalist, specializing in travel and popular culture, with the *Sydney Morning Herald*. He is also the owner and director of Australia's most comprehensive travel Internet site, walkabout.com.au. After living in Europe for seven years, Elder returned to Australia and committed to travelling and recording the history and attractions of his country. Since his return he has travelled extensively in all areas of Australia and has written a number of travel guides, including the New Holland publications *Globetrotter Guide to Sydney*, *Globetrotter Guide to Australia*, *Explore Queensland* and *Touring New South Wales*. His 1988 book *Blood*

on the Wattle, a history of the massacres of Australian Aboriginals, was recently nominated as one of the ten most influential works of Australian non-fiction.

PHILIP GAME has been an enthusiastic traveller since his student days in the early 1970s, although he does retain distant memories of a seventh-birthday excursion aboard the long-defunct Tasmanian Railways in 1959. He has worked as Australian vice-consul in the United Arab Emirates, and as a tour guide in Malaysia and Thailand, leading small groups moving by bus, communal taxi, longboat, elephant and of course, train. In 1995 he lived and travelled widely in the USA.

Philip Game's travel writing career was launched by the story of his experiences riding the now-defunct *Forsayth Mixed Goods 7A90* through the Queensland Outback in 1992. His articles have since been published in 28 countries, and many of them are catalogued on the web at www.travelgame.org.

JIM GILL was born in 1957 in Bedfordshire, England. He studied journalism and worked freelance for a number of years, both in print and in broadcasting, until he emigrated to Australia in 1989. En route he travelled by train from London to Nahodka, the first of six trips on the *Trans-Siberian*

Pierre Home-Douglas Anthony Lambert Peter Lemmey Lawrence Marshall

or *Trans-Mongolian Express*. Between 1992 and 2000 Jim worked as a journalist for the ABC in Perth, Western Australia and co-presenter for the *Breakfast Programme* for ABC radio. He left the latter to concentrate on freelance travel writing. Jim has travelled extensively, particularly by rail.

WALTER GLASER and his wife **CHERIE** (walterglaser@aol.com) are a truly global writing and photography team. Based in Melbourne, Australia, their articles on food, travel, humour, business and adventure have appeared in publications as diverse as the *Los Angeles Times*, *Manchester Guardian*, *Tatler Asia* and *South African Penthouse*. In the early 1990s Walter wrote much of *Fodor's Guide to Australia*.

Cherie, who has a great eye for colour and composition from her years as a Sogetsu Ikebana teacher, is now one of Australia's top travel photographers. Walter, who was educated at Melbourne's Wesley College and then at Melbourne University, started his career as an advertising executive, retiring from that field to pursue his great love for travel writing. They travel the world many times a year, returning to Australia to write about their experiences.

A native of Vancouver, British Columbia, **PIERRE HOME-DOUGLAS** has worked as a book editor and freelance travel writer since the late 1980s. His articles have ap-

peared in numerous Canadian and American newspapers and magazines on subjects including bicyling through Vermont, hiking in England, sailing up the Nile, and the time he travelled alone from Montreal to Florida at the age of 14 to witness the launch of Apollo 11. He has also written chapters for the Reader's Digest series *Explore America*. Pierre took his first long-distance train ride at the age of 4 when he, his mother, and 8-year-old brother travelled from Vancouver to Montreal. Since then, he has travelled extensively by rail through Europe and in the United States and continues to rely on the train daily to travel to his office in Montreal from his home in suburban Dorval.

ANTHONY LAMBERT has written 14 books about railways and travel, including *Switzerland by Rail* and *Explore Britain's Steam Railways*, and has contributed to the AA's *Train Journeys of the World* and the *Insight Guide to Pakistan*. He has also written on railway journeys for such newspapers and magazines as the *New York Times*, *Daily Telegraph*, *The Sunday Times*, *Wanderlust*, *Essentially America* and *World*. He was consultant editor to the nine-volume partwork *The World of Trains*, and has travelled on the railways of more than 40 countries.

He has talked to a wide range of audiences on railways and travel, including the Royal Geographical Society, of which he is a Fellow.

A native of Southern England, **PETER LEMMEY** developed a taste for rail travel early in life on the *Atlantic Coast Express*. Family holidays in Europe in the 1960s opened up the possibilities of exploring 'off the beaten track' by train, spurred on by travel writers like Bryan Morgan and P B Whitehouse who tempted many to cross the Channel to see for themselves.

In 1980 he made the first of many visits to the Indian subcontinent, where he sought out the local trains to explore some of the more remote and less-visited parts of India and Pakistan. In both countries his journeys were made even more rewarding by the hospitality of local railwaymen and by the cooperation of the railway administrations in furnishing him with permission for rides on the engines, railway accommodation in out-of-the-way spots, and on one or two occasions even special trains. At home he has contributed a number of articles about exotic train journeys to the travel press; he also helps run the Grand Junction Club, a dining club for those whose interests encompass railways, food and wine. He lives in north London and works in Whitehall.

LAWRENCE MARSHALL has had a passion for steam locomotives since 1940. After steam disappeared from British railways in 1968 he concentrated on the railways of India and made 25 visits to all parts of the sub-continent. His travels have also taken him to Pakistan, China, Cuba, Myanmar (Burma), North American and most of Europe.

Lawrence has written three books on the railways of Spain and a book covering his travels on the Indian narrow gauge. After finishing his national service he joined a British locomotive-building company in Leeds, but has spent most of his career working for Lloyds Bank, becoming a senior manager.

Born in 1930 and now retired, he enjoys book writing, photography, collecting railway memorabilia and modelling live steam engines. His wife Maureen accompanies him on most of his steam travels.

PETER NEVILLE-HADLEY is the author of two China travel guides: *China, The Silk Routes* and *Beijing*, both published by Cadogan Guides. He has been travelling regularly in China since 1986, and has crossed the country by rail several times. He spent a period in Beijing as editor of a magazine there, and writes on China and other Asian destinations for a number of magazines and newspapers in Europe, North America and Asia.

He also runs a moderated internet mailing list for the discussion of travel in China – new members welcome.

TOM SAVIO, general editor of this book as well as a major contributor to it, is a highly regarded photojournalist and broadcaster who specializes in luxury rail travel worldwide. His work has appeared in *Time*, *The New York Times* and a variety of North American newspapers, specialist publications and periodicals, as well as on radio and video. Tom is a member of the Lexington Group, the honorary society of railway journalists. He was also the editor of *Extraordinary Railway Journeys* (New Holland 2004).

SUSAN STORM was born in Prague in the Czech Republic, and her first journey was across the renowned Charles Bridge in a pram. She grew up in Cape Town, South Africa, and then in Europe and London, where she worked in television. She later emigrated to Perth, Western Australia, where she spread her literary and photographic wings, and began a succession of wild and wonderful photojournalistic experiences including glaciers in Chilean Patagonia, dragons on Komodo Island, witchetty grubs in Australia's outback, temples and markets in Southeast Asia, hot-air ballooning in Canberra, luxury train travel in Africa, sailing through the Mediterranean.

Susan is constantly on the move, toting her cameras and journals searching for stories for newspapers and magazines across the globe. Her latest home is Sydney, Australia, a city so glittering that she hopes she will never have to leave it permanently.

GRAHAM SIMMONS is a freelance travel writer and photographer based in Melbourne, Australia. He says his work is grudgingly accepted in a number of Australasian and international newspapers and magazines. Graham started travel writing in an attempt to get away from himself, but it didn't quite work. He says that travel is a cure for which there is no known disease.

Graham decided to visit Peru because it was a land of mystery in his homeland, Australia. The stories of the cruel Spanish *conquistadores* seemed totally at odds with the laidback lifestyle of Spanish migrants to Australia. At the same time, the treatment meted out to the native Indians of South America had strong parallels with the treatment of indigenous Australians. These conflicting messages seemed to warrant further investigation.

Peter Neville-Hadley   *Tom Savio*   *Susan Storm*   *Graham Simmons*

Booking &
General Information

THE CANADIAN
Bookings, Tel: +1 (888) 842 7245
Website: www.viarail.ca

THE COAST STARLIGHT
The Coast Starlight Organization
Amtrak
Tel: USA & Canada only, USA RAIL
(1 800 872 7245), rest of world only via
travel agent
www.amtrak.com

DURANGO & SILVERTON NARROW
GAUGE RAILROAD AND MUSEUM
479 Main, Durango, CO81301, USA
Tel: +1 (970) 247 2733
www.durangotrain.com/

CUMBRES & TOLTEC SCENIC RAILROAD
Tel: +1 (888) 286 2737
www.cumbrestoltec.com/

THE COPPER CANYON LINE
Booking
(In Chihuahua) Fax: +52 (1) 439 7212
(In El Fuerte)The gift shop at the Hotel
Posada del Hidalgo.

Information
Mr Enrique Dominguez Leon
Commercial Manager – Tourism Division
Ferromex, Chihuahua.
Tel: +52 (1) 439 7210
Fax: +52 (1) 439 7208
Email: chepe@ferromex.com.mx
www.coppercanyon-mexico.com

ROYAL SCOTSMAN
The Royal Scotsman Organization
UK: Tel: +44 (131) 555 1021
USA: 0800 323 7308 (only within USA) or
via Abercrombie & Kent tour agency.
Email: bookings@royalscotsman.co.uk
www.royalscotsman.com

LEEDS–CARLISLE
National Rail Enquiries, UK
Tel: +44 (8457) 48 49 50
Northern Spirit: Tel: +44 (870) 602 3322

FLÅM RAILWAY
Norges Statsbaner, Oslo, Norway
Tel: +47 81 50 08 88
Fax: +47 22 36 71 52
www.nsb.no

RHÔNE VALLEY
Chemin de Fer du Vivarais (Vivarais
railway): The railway is located in the
Doux Valley.
By road, take the A7, exiting at Tain.
By train, the closest stations are Valence
or Tain-Tournon, from where a bus goes
to Tournon. Trips are available from April
to November.
Tel: +33 (4) 78 28 83 34
Fax: +33 (4) 72 00 97 67

ALONG THE RHINE
Deutsche Bahn, Frankfurt-am-Main
Germany
Tel: +49 1805 99 66 33
www.bahn.de

GLACIER EXPRESS
UK
Switzerland Tourism, London
Tel: +44 800 100 200 30
Fax: +44 800 100 200 31
Email: stc@stlondon.com
www.MySwitzerland.com

USA
Switzerland Tourism, El Segundo
Tel: +1 (310) 335 0125
Fax: +1 (310) 335 0131
Email: stnewyork@switzerlandtourism.com

AL ANDALUS
Tel: +34 (91) 571 6692
Fax: +34 (91) 571 7482
Email: alandalus@alandalusexpreso.com
www.alandalusexpreso.com

EL TRANSCANTÁBRICO
Tel: +34 (91) 453 3806
Fax: +34 (91) 453 3824
Email: transcantabrico@feve.es
www.transcantabrico.feve.es

VENICE SIMPLON-ORIENT-EXPRESS
Venice Simplon-Orient-Express
London, UK
Tel: +44 (20) 7805 5060
Fax: +44 (20) 7805 5908
www.orient-express.com

TRANS-MONGOLIAN &TRANS-SIBERIAN

In Hong Kong:
Monkey Business
Tel: +852 2723 1376
www.monkeyshrine.com
In Perth, Western Australia:
The Travel Directors
Tel: +61 (8) 9322 5155

KHYBER PASS

Lahore–Peshawar:
PR Headquarters Booking and
Reservation Office, Pakistan Railways
Lahore.
Peshawar–Khyber Pass:
Sehrai Travels & Tours,
12 Saddar Road (opposite Green's Hotel),
Peshawar, Pakistan
Tel: +92 (91) 27 20 84
Fax: +92 (91) 27 20 85
Email: sehrai@psh.brain.net.pk

DARJEELING HIMALAYAN LINE

Central Reservation Office
New Delhi, India
Tel: +91 (11) 334 4680/1
www.indianrail.gov.in/

ROYAL ORIENT EXPRESS

Reservations
Central Reservation Office, New Delhi, India
Tel: +91 (11) 334 4680/1
www.indianrail.gov.in/
Abercrombie & Kent Overseas Ltd, UK:
email: info@abercrombiekent.co.uk
Tel: +44 (20) 7973 0484
Fax: +44 (20) 7730 9376
USA:
Tel: +1 (630) 954 2944
Fax: +1 (630) 954 3324
Email: info@abercrombiekent.com
www.abercrombiekent.com
Australia:
Tel: +61 (3) 9536 1800
Fax: +61 (3) 9536 1805

EASTERN & ORIENTAL EXPRESS

Venice Simplon-Orient-Express Ltd
London, UK
Tel: +44 (20) 7805 5100
Fax: +44 (20) 7805 5908
www.orient-express.com.

BEIJING TO HANOI

Beijing:
Beijing Jingte International Travel
Services Co.
With your back to the West station, walk
to the right (east) following the frontage
until you see a branch of the Construction
Bank of China. The bank is open 9–5 daily,
but it's best to call ahead with your passport number to make a booking. No English is spoken, so ask your hotel reception
staff to help.
Tel: +86 (10) 6398 9485,
or +86 (10) 63216541 (also fax)
Hanoi:
At the main railway station. English is spoken.

THE GHAN

Tel: 132-147 (within Australia),
Tel: +61 (8) 8213 4592 (overseas)
Fax: +61 (8) 8213 4490
Email: salesagent@gsr.com.au
www.gsr.com.au/index.htm

THE INDIAN PACIFIC

Adelaide, Australia
Tel: +61 (8) 8213 4444
Fax: +61 (8) 8213 4480
www.passengerrail.gsr.com.au/theindian-
pacific/ip_fares.htm
www.gsr.com.au/booking.htm

THE TRANZALPINE

From New Zealand:
Call free on 0800 802 802
Fax free on 0800 101 525
From outside New Zealand
Tel: +64 (4) 498 3303

ABOVE: *The Eastern and Oriental Express
travelling through exotic scenery in Thailand.*

Fax: +64 (4) 498 3090
www.tranzrailtravel.co.nz/
tranzScenic/theTranzAlpine/overview.asp

BLUE TRAIN

Tel: +27 (12) 334 8459
or toll free: 0800-117-715 (within South
Africa)
Email: bluetrain@transnet.co.za

PRIDE OF AFRICA

Rovos Rail Head Office, South Africa
Tel: +27 (12) 323 6052
Fax: +27 (12) 323 0843
Email: reservations@rovos.co.za
www.rovos.co.za

DISCLAIMER

The information supplied here is based
on the suggestions of the authors and
the research of the publisher, but is in
no way an endorsement of any of the
listed parties.

Index

BOLD NUMBERS REPRESENT PHOTOGRAPHS

PHOTOGRAPHIC CREDITS

Photographers:

AA = Al Andalus
AW = Alan Wild
AL = Anthony Lambert
CB = Colin Boocock
CI = Corbis Images

DR = David Rogers
DW = David Wall
EOEC = Eastern & Oriental Express Company
EC = Eugeni Casanova
GC = Gerald Cubitt
GS = Graham Simmons
GSR = Great Southern Railways
IB = Image Bank
JG = Jim Gill
JMA = John & Mary Lou Aitchison
JT = John Tickner
LC = Liz Crossley
LM = Laurie Marshall

OE = Orient-Express
PG = Philip Game
PL = Peter Lemmey
PM = Peter Mertz
PNH = Peter Neville-Hadley
RR = Rovos Rail
SB = Steve Barry
SS = Susan Storm
TBAL = The Bridgeman Art Library
TS = Tom Savio
VRC = VIA Rail Canada
WCG = Walter & Cherie Glaser

Endpapers	TBAL	42		OE	90		JG	126–127	DW
2	PL	43		GS	92	tl/bl	EC	128	GSR
5	PM	44–45		PM	93	tl	JG	129	PG
6–7	CB	46–49		TS		tr	EC	130	GSR
8–11	CI	50–52		JT	94		JG	131	PG
12	PL	54–55		AW	95		EC	132	GSR
14–15	AL	56		CB	96–99		PL	133	SS
16	PM	57		AW	100		LM	134	GSR
17	TS	58–61		PL	101–103		JT	136	DW
18	PM	62		IB	104–109		WCG	137	SS
19	SB	63–69		CB	110–111		TS	139	DW
20	VRC	70–74		EC	112		GC	140–141	DR
21–23	PM	75		AA	114		TS	142	SS
24–27	TS	76–77		EC	115		GC	143	DR
28–29	AL	78–82		CB	116		TS	144–145	SS
30	SB	84–85		PM	117		PG	146	RR
31–33	AL	87		PL	118–121		PNH	147	LC
34–37	PG	88		JMA	122–123		PG	148–151	RR
38–39, 157	AL	89		CB	124–125		PNH	156	EOEC

ACKNOWLEDGMENTS

Thanks to Malcolm Andrews and Seychelle Harding at VIA Rail, Cliff Black at Amtrak, Chris Hillyard, RVM, of the *Royal Train*, Pippa Isbell and Joanna Boyen at Orient-Express, The Wolsztyn Experience, Capt. Simon Pooley and the 'Baroness' Yvonne. Also to the authors for their patient attention to our many queries, and particularly to Tom Savio the Railway Baron for sharing his great experience and intimate knowledge of railway travel, and not least for his unfailing sense of humour.